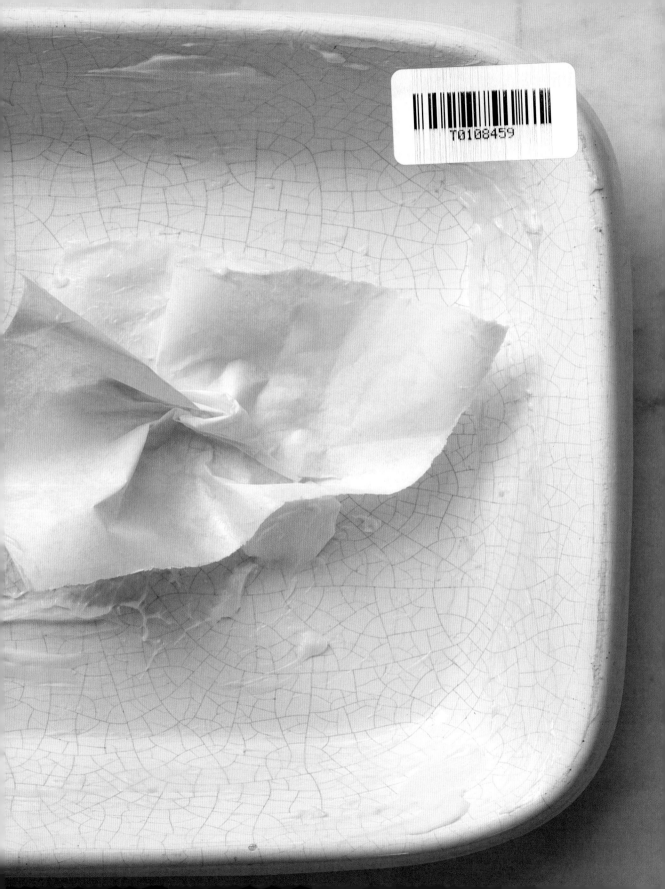

HOME-COOKED
comforts

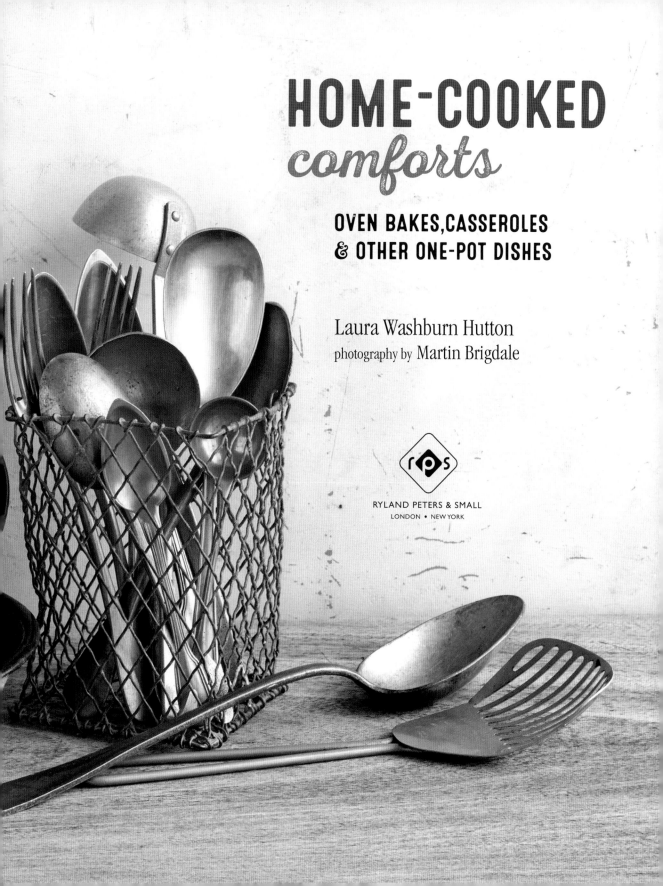

HOME-COOKED
comforts

OVEN BAKES, CASSEROLES
& OTHER ONE-POT DISHES

Laura Washburn Hutton

photography by Martin Brigdale

RYLAND PETERS & SMALL
LONDON • NEW YORK

Designer Steve Painter
Editorial Director Julia Charles
Head of Production
 Patricia Harrington
Art Director Leslie Harrington
Publisher Cindy Richards

Food Stylist Linda Tubby
Prop Stylist Roisin Nield
Indexer Hilary Bird

First published in 2010.
This edition published in 2020
by Ryland Peters & Small
20–21 Jockey's Fields, London
WC1R 4BW
and
341 E 116th St, New York
NY 10029
www.rylandpeters.com

10 9 8 7 6 5 4 3 2 1

Text copyright © Laura Washburn
Hutton 2010, 2020.
Design and photographs copyright
© Ryland Peters & Small 2010,
2020.

ISBN: 978-1-78879-283-7

A CIP record for this book is
available from the British Library.

US Library of Congress cataloging-
in-publication data has been applied
for.

Printed and bound in China.

Notes
• Both British (Metric) and
American (Imperial plus US cup)
measurements are included in
these recipes for your convenience,
however it is important to work
with one set of measurements only
and not alternate between the two.
• All spoon measurements are level,
unless otherwise specified.
• Traditional Parmesan is made
with animal rennet and therefore
not suitable for vegetarians so use
a vegetarian substitute if preferred.
• All eggs are medium (UK) or large
(US), unless specified as large, in
which case US extra-large should be
used. Uncooked or partially cooked
eggs should not be served to the very
old, frail, young children, pregnant
women or those with compromised
immune systems.
• When a recipe calls for the grated
zest of citrus fruit, buy unwaxed fruit
and wash well before using.
• Ovens should be preheated to
the specified temperature. Recipes
in this book were tested using a
regular oven. If using a fan-assisted
oven, follow the manufacturer's
instructions for adjusting the
temperatures given.

contents

The comforts of home cooking

On any given, usually frantic, day the thought of something bubbling away in the kitchen can seem like shelter in a storm. The pace of life can on occasions be frenetic for everyone, everywhere, it seems. I often retreat to my pots and pans, seeking solace in the stockpot. What better way to take some speed off the modern pace of life by spending just a little time in the kitchen, making something warming and comforting?

In this busy world, it is often hard to find time for the simple things, such as preparing a nice meal for family and friends. Even as someone with food preparation in my job description, as a working parent, I struggled to find the time more often than I care to admit. But the recipes presented in this book are intended to offer respite for the harried. They are designed to make it simple to slow down and savour something delicious, with main courses that can go straight from hob or oven to the table. Written with busy people in mind, many of the recipes can be quickly assembled, then left to simmer or bake, leaving time for other occupations and most can be made in advance so you can cook when you do have time, for enjoyment later on. Most are as suitable for midweek suppers as they are for weekend entertaining and, because times continue to change, some of the more flexible recipes offer helpful suggestions for vegetarian variations.

But spending time in the kitchen is not only good for our frame of mind, it can be good for our bodies. Home-made food can be so much more wholesome, especially when meals are prepared from scratch. So ease of preparation is not the only consideration; the recipes in this book also offer a way to put nutritious food on the table. Personally, I take great comfort in knowing what goes into the food on my plate and I don't like to leave the cooking to a factory assembly line. Preparing a square meal is so much simpler than you think, why do anything else? For the most part, each recipe in this book is a one-pot meal, often requiring little more than a crisp green salad and some crusty bread to complete composition. Easy, delicious, nutritious; it's hard to do better than that.

These recipes also offer plenty of variety for when you want to spice things up. I always turn to my cookbooks to get out of my routine so I have tried to make this a collection of dishes inspired by cuisines from around the world. Alongside traditional family fare, there are also recipes for curries, Oriental dishes, Moroccan tagines and some favourites from the American South-west. Not restaurant food, but the kinds of dishes eaten at home, making them straightforward for any cook to prepare regardless of skill, using ingredients that can be found in most supermarkets. So go on, home cook some comfort today.

meat

black bean and chorizo chili

This is not mouth-searingly hot like some recipes. Quite the opposite, and the addition of chorizo adds another layer of flavour but not necessarily heat. Serve with boiled rice and/or warmed tortillas, and a simple salad of sliced avocados sprinkled with lime juice and olive oil. If you have any leftovers, this chili also makes a nice alternative filling for the Vegetable Enchiladas on page 114.

250 g/9 oz. chorizo, finely chopped

2–3 tablespoons vegetable oil

1 large onion, diced

4 (bell) peppers, mixed red, yellow and orange, diced

2 celery sticks/stalks, with leaves, diced

2 teaspoons dried chilli/ hot red pepper flakes

½ teaspoon cayenne pepper (optional)

2½ teaspoons ground cumin

2 teaspoons dried oregano

2 garlic cloves, finely chopped

250 g/9 oz. minced/ground beef

250 ml/1 cup red wine

500 ml/2 cups beef stock

1 bay leaf

400-g/14-oz. can chopped tomatoes

2 x 400-g/14-oz.-cans black beans, drained

a handful of fresh coriander/ cilantro leaves, chopped

2 fresh red chillies/chiles, sliced and deseeded (optional)

sea salt

sour cream, to serve

rice or flour tortillas, to serve

Serves 4

Put the chorizo in a small saucepan and set over medium heat. Cook until browned then transfer the chorizo to a plate lined with kitchen paper/paper towels and then set aside.

Heat 2 tablespoons of the oil in a large saucepan/pot. Add the onions and cook for 2–3 minutes, until soft. Add the (bell) peppers and celery, season with a little salt, and cook for a further 3–5 minutes, until soft. Stir in the chilli/hot red pepper flakes, cayenne (if using), cumin, oregano and garlic and cook, stirring, for 1 minute. Add the minced/ground beef and cook for 5–7 minutes, stirring occasionally, until browned. Season with a little more salt.

Add the wine and cook for 1 minute, then stir in the stock, bay leaf, tomatoes and beans. Cover, reduce the heat and simmer for 15 minutes. Taste for seasoning and chilli/ chile heat and adjust as necessary. Continue simmering, uncovered, for a further 20–30 minutes.

When ready to serve, stir in the coriander/cilantro. Scatter over the slices fresh chillies/chiles (if using) and serve the sour cream on the side. Rice and/or warmed flour tortillas make a good accompaniment.

Hungarian goulash

This recipe was given to me by a Hungarian friend, who is an exceptional cook. It took a few tries to get mine to taste as good as hers. Apparently, she makes it just like her grandmother does, but it was very difficult to extract the method for their 'secret' touch. It has something to do with feeling; theirs is surely superlative. She did explain that Hungarians always cook with generous doses of spice and perhaps add more salt than is recommended so feel free to do the same. This is traditionally served with wide ribbon egg noodles but works well with pasta such as tagliatelle.

1 tablespoon vegetable oil

2 onions, diced

1 red (bell) pepper, deseeded and diced

1 green (bell) pepper, deseeded and diced

1 teaspoon caraway seeds

2 generous teaspoons paprika, sweet or hot, or half and half

750 g/1 lb. 10 oz. stewing beef, cut into small cubes

3 large ripe tomatoes, peeled, cored, deseeded and chopped

1 tablespoon tomato purée/paste

3 carrots, diced

375 ml/1½ cups beef stock

2 bay leaves

400-g/14-oz. can kidney beans, drained

a large handful of fresh flat-leaf parsley leaves, chopped

sea salt and freshly ground black pepper

wide egg noodles or ribbon pasta, to serve

Serves 4

Heat the oil in a large saucepan/pot. Add the onions and (bell) peppers and cook until soft. Season with a littlesalt and add the caraway seeds and paprika. Cook for 1 minute. Add the cubed beef. Cook, stirring occasionally, for 2–3 minutes, until browned. Season with a little more salt if liked.

Add the tomatoes, tomato purée/paste, carrots, stock and bay leaves, and season lightly. Simmer, uncovered, for at least 40 minutes. Add the kidney beans and cook for 10 minutes more (do not be tempted to add the beans any earlier as they will become tough if overcooked).

Sprinkle with the choppedparsley and serve spooned over egg noodles or ribbon pasta.

steak, leek and mushroom pie with Guinness

Pies are a wonderful thing. They look and taste fantastic, and are really straightforward to make, especially if you leave out the bottom layer of pastry, which I always do. Serve with plenty of creamy mashed potatoes and peas, if liked.

1 tablespoon vegetable oil

700 g/1 lb. 9 oz. stewing beef, cut into bite-sized pieces

2 trimmed leeks (about 500 g/ 1 lb. 2 oz.), sliced into rounds

1 onion, coarsely chopped

2 large carrots, peeled and diced

250 g/9 oz. mushrooms, coarsely chopped

100 g/3½ oz. bacon (about 3 rashers/slices), chopped

1 teaspoon dried thyme

2 garlic cloves, crushed

2 tablespoons plain/all-purpose flour

330 ml/scant 1½ cups Guinness or other dark dry stout

2 tablespoons Worcestershire sauce

1 bay leaf

a large handful of fresh flat-leaf parsley leaves, chopped

375-g/13-oz. pack ready-rolled puff pastry, defrosted if frozen

melted butter or milk, to brush

sea salt and freshly ground black pepper

a large flameproof casserole dish
a 30 x 20-cm/11¾ x 8-inch baking dish

Serves 4–6

Preheat the oven to 160°C (325°F) Gas 3.

Heat the oil in a large flameproof casserole dish. Add the beef and cook, stirring, for 2–3 minutes, until just browned. Remove the meat from the casserole dish, season and set aside.

Add the leeks, onion and carrots to the pan, adding a little more oil if necessary. Cook over low heat for about 3 minutes, until softened. Add the mushrooms, bacon and thyme and cook for a further 2–3 minutes. Season well. Add the garlic and cook for 1 minute.

Return the beef to the casserole dish, add the flour, stir to coat the meat in the flour and cook for 2–3 minutes. Pour in the Guinness and Worcestershire sauce. Add the bay leaf and parsley and pour in sufficient cold water to just cover. Stir to mix, cover with a lid and bake in the preheated oven for about 1½ hours.

Remove the casserole dish from the oven and increase the oven temperature to 200°C (400°F) Gas 6.

Transfer the beef mixture to the baking dish. Unroll the pastry and use to cover the pie filling. It should look rustic, so fold over the edges and crimp roughly with your fingers. Using a sharp knife, and starting at the top edge, make lengthways slits on the diagonal, in stripes about ½ cm/⅜ inch apart, all the way across. Brush with melted butter or milk and bake in the preheated oven for about 25–30 minutes, until golden. Serve immediately with mashed potatoes and peas on the side.

beef and courgette gratin

It's not possible to have too many recipes for minced/ground meat. The goats' cheese gives this dish a tangy lift but, as the flavour is not for everyone, mature/sharp Cheddar is a good alternative. Ideal for feeding a crowd, it makes a change from lasagne. Serve with a salad and crusty bread.

1 onion, finely chopped

about 125 ml/½ cup olive oil

1 teaspoon each dried thyme and dried oregano

¼ teaspoon dried chilli/ hot red pepper flakes

2 garlic cloves, crushed

125 ml/½ cup dry white wine

500 g/1 lb. 2 oz. minced/ ground beef

400-g/14-oz. can chopped tomatoes

a pinch of sugar

1.8 kg/4 lb. courgettes/zucchini (about 6), sliced into 1-cm/ ½-inch rounds

225-g/8-oz. crème fraîche

60 g/2 oz. soft goats' cheese

110 g/3½ oz. Gruyère, grated

1–2 tablespoons milk

sea salt and freshly ground black pepper

a 25 x 20-cm/9¾ x 8-inch deep-sided baking dish

Serves 4–6

In a large frying pan/skillet, add the onions and about 1 tablespoon of the oil. Cook over medium heat for about 3–5 minutes, until soft. Stir in the thyme, oregano, chilli/hot red pepper flakes and garlic and cook, stirring, for about 1 minute. Add the wine, cook for 1 further minute, then add the beef. Cook for 5–8 minutes, stirring occasionally, until the beef is browned. Stir in the tomatoes and sugar and season well. Reduce the heat, cover and simmer gently for at least 15 minutes.

Preheat the oven to 200°C (400°F) Gas 6.

Meanwhile, prepare the courgettes/zucchini. Line a tray with kitchen paper/paper towels. Working in batches, heat some of the oil in a large non-stick frying pan/skillet. When hot, add the courgette/zucchini rounds and fry, in a single layer. When just golden, turn and brown the other side. Transfer each batch to the lined tray.

Stir 2 tablespoons of the crème fraîche into the beef mixture. Put the remaining crème fraîche in a bowl, crumble in the goats' cheese and season with salt and pepper. Mix well. Set aside.

To assemble, arrange one-third of the courgettes/zucchini in an even layer on the bottom of the baking dish. Sprinkle with salt and one-third of the Gruyère. Top with half of the beef mixture, spread evenly. Repeat the courgette/ zucchini and beef layer. Finish with a final courgette/ zucchini layer. Season with salt, then spread with an even layer of the crème fraîche topping. Sprinkle over the remaining Gruyère. Bake in the preheated oven for about 30 minutes, until the top is golden brown. Serve with a mixed salad and crusty bread.

Asian beef braise with pak choi/bok choy

A different kind of beef stew, this recipe has flavours of the Orient but is easy to make at home with ordinary Western utensils. If you can find cubes of frozen chopped ginger at your supermarket, they will come in handy here, or in any recipe, which is why I like to keep them around. Serve this with any kind of Oriental noodle – egg noodles will do the trick, or try something more unusual like Japanese soba noodles or thick Ho Fun noodles.

2 tablespoons vegetable oil

1 kg/2 lb. 7 oz. braising steak, cut into bite-sized pieces

1 garlic clove, crushed

1 large shallot, sliced

25-g/1-oz. piece of fresh ginger, peeled and grated (about 1 tablespoon)

750 ml/3 cups beef stock

125 ml/½ cup Chinese rice wine

125 ml/½ cup hoisin sauce

¼ teaspoon ground cumin

1 star anise

1 fresh red chilli/chile, sliced

freshly squeezed juice of 1 tangerine (or ½ an orange)

1 teaspoon runny honey

4–6 pak choi/bok choy

your choice of noodles, to serve

Serves 4

Heat the oil in a large saucepan/pot. Add the steak and cook until browned. Transfer to a plate, season with salt and set aside.

Add the garlic, shallot and ginger to the saucepan and cook, stirring constantly for 1 minute. Add the stock, rice wine, hoisin sauce, cumin, star anise, chilli/chile, tangerine juice and honey. Stir to blend and bring to the boil. Return the steak to the saucepan, reduce the heat and simmer very gently, uncovered, for 1–1½ hours, until the meat is tender. Taste and adjust the seasoning.

Core the pak choi/bok choy. Cut the white part into 1.5-cm/⅝-inch slices; leave the greens large or cut in half. Add the white part to the saucepan, increase the heat and cook until just tender, 3–4 minutes. Add the greens and cook until just wilted, about 2–3 minutes more. Serve immediately with cooked noodles of your choice.

Thai red beef curry

This is a truly straightforward curry recipe. There are many brands of curry paste available, some better than others, but if you find a good one, this will taste remarkably authentic. In reality, you could simply stop at the curry paste and coconut milk, but I like to jazz up the ready-made sauce with even more lemongrass and ginger. And, the fish sauce and palm sugar give the finished dish more depth. Use this as a blueprint recipe for any Thai red curry and experiment with different ingredients in place of the beef. Boneless chicken or prawns/shrimp work well, as do a mixture of vegetables such as baby sweetcorn, aubergine/eggplant, sweet potato and broccoli. Serve with basmati rice, either steamed or boiled.

1 tablespoon vegetable oil

800 g/1 lb. 12 oz. sirloin steak, sliced into thin strips

4 tablespoons Thai red curry paste

2 x 400-g/14-oz. cans coconut milk

½ lemongrass stalk, white part only, very finely chopped

1–2 tablespoons Thai fish sauce, to taste

30-g/1-oz. piece of fresh ginger, peeled and grated
(about 1½ tablespoons)

1 tablespoon palm sugar or runny honey

300 g/10½ oz. green beans, cut into 3-cm/1¼-inch lengths

steamed basmati rice, to serve

Serves 4

Heat the oil in a large saucepan/pot. Add the beef and cook for 2–3 minutes, stirring, until just browned. Add the curry paste and continue cooking for 1–2 minutes, stirring occasionally to coat the meat.

Add the coconut milk, lemongrass, 1 tablespoon of the fish sauce, ginger and sugar. Stir well, reduce the heat, and simmer gently for 15 minutes. Taste and add the remaining tablespoon of fish sauce if necessary. Continue simmering, uncovered, for about 15 minutes more.

Add the green beans, part cover and simmer gently for about 10 minutes more until the beans are just tender. Serve immediately with plenty of steamed basmati rice.

tamale pie

1 tablespoon vegetable oil

1 onion, finely chopped

1 green (bell) pepper, finely chopped

500 g/1 lb. 2 oz. minced/ground pork or beef

2 teaspoons chilli/chili powder

1 teaspoon ground cumin

½ teaspoon allspice

400-g/14-oz. can kidney beans or black beans, drained

400-g/14-oz. can chopped tomatoes

100 g/1 cup stoned/pitted black olives, sliced

150 g/1 cup sweetcorn kernels

1 tablespoon Worcestershire sauce

Tabasco sauce (optional)

sea salt and freshly ground black pepper

For the topping

300 g/2¼ cups plain/all-purpose flour

300 g/2 cups cornmeal

2 teaspoons baking powder

¼ teaspoon salt

a pinch of sugar

3 tablespoons melted butter

180 ml/¾ cup milk

1 egg, beaten

1 small fresh green chilli/chile, very finely chopped

45 g/1½ oz. Cheddar, grated

a 30 x 20-cm/11¾ x 8-inch baking dish

Serves 4–6

This pie has a cornbread topping, instead of the traditional masa harina, which is not always easy to obtain. It's easy to prepare and is a great recipe to fiddle. You can use leftover roast meat instead of minced/ground meat, either pork or beef, or both. If you have an abundant supply of fresh chillies/chiles, try some instead of the green (bell) pepper, or simply add as well. A handful of chopped jalapeños from a jar are good to add a real kick. Serve with sour cream and a salad of thinly sliced tomatoes and red onions, dressed with oil, lime juice and a sprinkling of fresh coriander/cilantro.

Preheat the oven to 190°C (375°F) Gas 5.

Heat the oil in a frying pan/skillet. Add the onion and green (bell) pepper and cook for about 5 minutes, until soft. Season and add the minced/ground pork or beef, chilli/chili powder, cumin and allspice. Cook, stirring often, until browned.

Stir in the beans, tomatoes, olives, sweetcorn and Worcestershire sauce. Reduce the heat and simmer, uncovered, for about 10–15 minutes.

Meanwhile, prepare the topping. Put the flour, cornmeal, baking powder, salt and sugar in a bowl and stir to combine. Stir in the melted butter, milk and egg and stir just until blended. Stir in the chilli/chile and cheese. Add an extra spoonful of milk if the mixture seems dry.

Taste the meat mixture and adjust the seasoning if necessary. Add a splash of Tabasco if it is not hot enough. Spoon into the baking dish and spread evenly. Drop the cornmeal mixture in spoonfuls on top, spreading evenly to cover.

Bake in the preheated oven for about 30 minutes, until the topping is golden brown. Serve immediately.

Vegetarian option: Replace the meat with an additional can of beans and add 1–2 diced courgettes/zucchini, cooked along with the onion and (bell) pepper.

braised pot roast with red wine, rosemary and bay leaves

This is the sort of food that makes you long for cold wintry days, when it is nice to stay indoors and simmer something slowly – heating the kitchen and filling the house with rich, warming aromas. It also has appeal for the lazy spendthrift as preparation is minimal and the cut of meat is inexpensive. There are several nice accompaniments for this: you could serve creamy mashed potatoes, soft polenta or even macaroni baked in cream with plenty of Parmesan.

1.2 kg/2 lb. 9 oz. braising joint, such as beef brisket, tied

2 tablespoons olive oil

1 onion, halved and thinly sliced

2 celery sticks/stalks, thinly sliced

1 large carrot, thinly sliced and cut into half-moons

4 garlic cloves, peeled and sliced

150 g/5½ oz. pancetta, very finely chopped

750 ml/3¼ cups robust red wine, preferably Italian

400-g/14-oz. can chopped tomatoes

1 bay leaf, 2 large sprigs fresh rosemary, several sprigs fresh parsley, all firmly tied together in a bundle

3–4 tablespoons capers in brine, drained (optional)

sea salt and freshly ground black pepper

a large flameproof casserole dish

Serves 6

Preheat the oven to 180°C (350°F) Gas 4.

Heat the oil in a large flameproof casserole dish. Add the beef and cook for about 8–10 minutes, until browned on all sides. Transfer the beef to a plate, season all over with salt and set aside.

Add the onion, celery and carrot to the casserole dish and cook, stirring often, until browned. Add the garlic and pancetta and cook for 1 minute. Season, then add the wine and tomatoes and bring to the boil. Boil for 1 minute, then add the herb bundle. Return the browned beef to the casserole dish.

Cover and transfer to the preheated oven. After 1½ hours, remove the casserole dish from the oven and turn the beef over. Pour in some water if the liquid has reduced too much and add the capers, if using. Return to the oven and cook for a further 1½ hours, until the meat is tender.

Serve in slices with the sauce and vegetables spooned over the top and with the accompaniment of your choice.

meatloaf

A free-form meatloaf has a few advantages. There is more browned surface on the top, which is the part I like the most, and it looks nicer. This American classic simply must be served with mashed potatoes and gravy, and leftovers make the perfect sandwich filling.

1 onion, coarsely chopped

2 garlic cloves

1 celery stick/stalk, coarsely chopped

leaves from a small bunch of fresh flat-leaf parsley

2 tablespoons olive oil

750 g/1 lb. 10 oz. minced/ ground beef

350 g/12 oz. minced/ ground pork

2 eggs, beaten

2 tablespoons milk

100 g/1¼ cups fresh breadcrumbs (see note)

1 teaspoon dried thyme

2 teaspoons salt

½ teaspoon ground white pepper

1 teaspoon paprika

60 ml/4 tablespoons chilli/ chili sauce or tomato ketchup

2–3 bay leaves, plus extra to garnish

5–6 streaky bacon rashers/slices

sea salt and freshly ground black pepper

a heavy baking sheet or shallow roasting pan

Serves 6–8

Preheat the oven to 180°C (350°F) Gas 4.

Combine the onion, garlic, celery and parsley in a food processor and pulse until minced.

Transfer the mixture to a frying pan/skillet, add the oil and cook over low heat for 5–7 minutes, until soft. Transfer to a large bowl and add the beef, pork, eggs, milk, breadcrumbs, thyme, salt, pepper, paprika and chilli/chili sauce. Mix with your hands until well blended.

Form the mixture into an oval loaf shape, as if you were making bread. Put the bay leaves in the middle of the baking sheet and place the meatloaf on top. Arrange the bacon rashers/slices on top, at equal intervals.

Bake in the preheated oven for about 1½ hours, until browned and cooked through. Do check the meatloaf regularly and baste with the pan juices to keep it moist. Serve with mashed potatoes and gravy.

Note: The best way to obtain fresh breadcrumbs is to use the end pieces from a sliced loaf, wholemeal or white but nothing with seeds. Simply tear into smaller pieces and put in the bowl of a food processor and processor to obtain crumbs. (The food processor is required for the onions in this recipe as well but do the breadcrumbs first because they are a dry ingredient.)

oven-braised lamb shanks with potatoes and tomatoes

Anything that contains an entire bottle of wine cannot possibly be bad, and this is surely proof. It is based on a recipe for leg of lamb which cooks for seven hours. In the interest of using less energy, I have changed the cut of meat and reduced the cooking time, with great success. This is incredibly simple and utterly satisfying. And although it is rustic, it is impressive, so perfect for entertaining. To keep with the energy saving theme, serve by candlelight.

2 tablespoons olive oil

4 lamb shanks

3 onions, quartered

5 carrots, coarsely chopped

6 garlic cloves, sliced

4 anchovy fillets, finely chopped (optional)

750 ml/3 cups dry white wine

1 bay leaf, 1 large sprig of fresh thyme, 1 large sprig of fresh rosemary, several sprigs of fresh parsley, all firmly tied together in a bundle

1 kg/2 lb. 3 oz. new potatoes, quartered

6 fresh plum tomatoes, cored and coarsely chopped

sea salt and freshly ground black pepper

a large flameproof casserole dish

Serves 4

Preheat the oven to 150°C (300°F) Gas 2.

Heat the oil in a flameproof casserole dish. Add the lamb shanks and cook for about 7–10 minutes, until browned all over, turning halfway through. Transfer the lamb shanks to a dish, season generously with salt and set aside.

Add the onions and carrots to the casserole dish and cook for 3–5 minutes, until just browned. Add the garlic and anchovies, if using, and cook for 1 minute. Season well and add the wine. Bring to the boil and cook for 1 minute. Return the lamb shanks to the casserole dish and add the herb bundle, burying it in the liquid. Add water if necessary; the lamb should be almost completely submerged in liquid. Cover and cook in the preheated oven for 2 hours, checking occasionally, to ensure the liquid does not reduce too much.

After 2 hours, top up with water if the liquid has greatly reduced, then add the potatoes and tomatoes and a good pinch of salt. Cook for 1 hour. Remove from the oven, taste and adjust the seasoning if necessary. Remove the herb bundle before serving.

moussaka

Some recipes for this traditional Greek dish call for potatoes alongside aubergines/eggplant, and some have potatoes only. This one is all aubergine/eggplant. Another departure here is the yoghurt topping in place of the classic béchamel sauce. The result is a lighter finished dish, less toil for the cook and an even better flavour, if I do say so myself! This improves over time so is best made a day in advance, refrigerated and baked when ready to serve.

1 onion, chopped

4–5 tablespoons olive oil

500 g/1 lb 2 oz. minced/ground lamb

2 garlic cloves, finely chopped

½ teaspoon ground allspice

¼ teaspoon ground cinnamon

2 teaspoons dried oregano

125 ml/½ cup red wine

2 x 400-g/14-oz. cans chopped tomatoes

1 bay leaf, plus extra to garnish

a pinch of sugar

3 medium aubergines/eggplant, sliced into 1-cm/½-inch rounds

sea salt and freshly ground black pepper

For the topping

350 ml/generous 1½ cups Greek yoghurt

2 eggs, beaten

150 g/5½ oz. feta, crumbled

a large handful of fresh mint leaves, chopped

3 tablespoons freshly grated Parmesan

a 30 x 20-cm/11¾ x 8-inch baking dish

Serves 6

Combine the onion and 1 tablespoon of the oil in a large frying pan/skillet. Cook the onion for about 3–5 minutes, until soft. Add the lamb, season well and cook, stirring, for about 5 minutes, until browned. Add the garlic, allspice, cinnamon and oregano and cook for 1 minute. Add the wine and cook for 1 minute more. Add the tomatoes, bay leaf and sugar and mix. Let simmer gently, uncovered, while you prepare the aubergines/eggplant.

Preheat the oven to 200°C (400°F) Gas 6.

Heat a few tablespoons of the oil in a large non-stick frying pan/skillet. Add the aubergine/eggplant slices in a single layer and cook to brown slightly. Using tongs, turn and cook the other sides, then transfer to kitchen paper/paper towels to drain. Work in batches, adding more oil as necessary, until all the aubergine/eggplant slices are browned.

In a bowl, combine the yoghurt, eggs and feta and mix well with a fork until blended. Season well with salt and pepper and stir in the mint. Set aside.

To assemble the moussaka, arrange half of the lamb mixture on the bottom of the baking dish. Top with half of the aubergine/eggplant slices. Repeat once more. Spread the yoghurt mixture on top and level the surface. Sprinkle with the Parmesan and decorate with bay leaves.

Bake in the preheated oven for about 40–50 minutes, until golden brown and bubbling. Serve immediately.

spiced lamb tagine with prunes

Tagines may sound exotic, but they couldn't be easier to prepare as they are in effect a one-pot casserole. This recipe is a perfect example. It is simple and satisfying, perfect as a weeknight supper but equally suited for entertaining. Serve with couscous and a watercress salad dressed with extra virgin olive oil and freshly squeezed orange juice.

2 onions

2 tablespoons olive oil

1 teaspoon ground turmeric

1 teaspoon ground ginger

½ teaspoon freshly ground black pepper

a pinch of saffron threads

1 teaspoon ground cumin

½ teaspoon ground cinnamon

1 kg/2 lb. 3 oz. stewing lamb, cut into bite-sized pieces

a small bunch of fresh coriander/cilantro, firmly tied into a bundle with string

225 g/1¾ cups stoned/pitted soft prunes

2 tablespoons runny honey

sea salt and freshly ground black pepper

couscous, to serve

Serves 4

Finely chop 1 of the onions either by grating it on the coarse side of a grater or processing in a food processor. Put it in a large saucepan/pot or flameproof casserole dish.

Add the oil, spices and lamb. Cook over low heat for 2–3 minutes, stirring to coat the lamb in oil, until the mixture becomes aromatic. Season well with salt. Pour in sufficient water just to cover and add the coriander/cilantro bundle. Reduce the heat, cover and simmer gently for 1½ hours.

Halve the remaining onion and slice into thin half moon slices. When the lamb is tender, remove with a slotted spoon and transfer to a dish. Cover and keep warm.

Add the sliced onion, prunes and honey to the liquid in the saucepan/casserole dish. Cover and cook for about 15 minutes, until the onion is tender. Remove the lid and simmer for about 5–8 minutes to reduce the sauce slightly. Return the lamb to the pan and toss well. Serve spooned over some couscous and with a watercress salad on the side, if liked.

Mediterranean stuffed onions with rice

Onions make a nifty, and tasty, container for the gently spiced lamb filling. This dish is a fantastic all-season meal; in winter, serve it hot for something comforting and satisfying. When it's warmer, this can be served at room temperature, accompanied by a mixed leaf salad. Do be sure to season the stuffing mixture well or the finished dish will be bland.

8 large red or white onions, peeled if liked

2–3 tablespoons olive oil

500 g/1 lb. 2 oz. minced/ground lamb

2 garlic cloves, crushed

1 heaped tablespoon tomato purée/paste

½ teaspoon ground cinnamon

2 tablespoons finely chopped fresh dill

2 tablespoons finely chopped fresh mint leaves

125 ml/½ cup dry white wine

300 g/1½ cups brown rice

1 egg, beaten

100 g/1¼ cups fresh breadcrumbs
(see note on page 26)

sea salt and freshly ground black pepper

a baking dish, large enough to take all the onions in a single layer

Serves 4

Slice the tops and bottoms off of the onions, taking only a little at the root end and more at the top. Use a melon baller to scoop out the insides, leaving 2–3 layers of the outer onion as a shell. Put the scooped-out onion flesh in a food processor and process until finely chopped.

Put 1 tablespoon of the oil in a large frying pan/skillet and add 4 tablespoons of the chopped onions (the remainder can be frozen for use in other recipes). Cook for 3–5 minutes, until soft. Add the lamb, season well, and cook for 5–7 minutes, stirring to break up the meat. Stir in the garlic, tomato purée/paste, cinnamon, dill, mint and wine and cook for 2–3 minutes, stirring. Taste and adjust the seasoning. Remove from the heat and let cool.

Preheat the oven to 200°C (400°F) Gas 6.

Add the rice in an even layer in the bottom of the baking dish. Brush the inside of the onion shells with oil and sprinkle with salt.

When the stuffing is cool enough to handle, stir in the breadcrumbs and egg and about 2–3 tablespoons water. The mixture should be soft, but not soupy. Spoon the mixture into the onion shells, filling all the way to the top, mounding only slightly. Arrange the filled onions on top of the rice and brush the outsides with oil. Pour about 500 ml/2 cups water into the dish.

Bake in the preheated oven for 1–1½ hours, until the rice is cooked and tender and the onions are browned. Keep an eye on the rice and begin testing it after 1 hour in the oven. You may need to add more water. Serve immediately or let cool to room temperature and serve with a mixed green salad on the side.

meatball tagine

This is an unusual but traditional Moroccan recipe. When prepared in a tagine (cooking vessel), the eggs are cooked in the dish with the meatballs, on top of the sauce. This recipe cooks the eggs separately, allowing for preparation in an ordinary straight-sided frying pan/skillet. If you feel the need to add something green, add some frozen peas with the meatballs. This is not traditional, but tasty. Serve with bread to mop up the aromatic sauce.

½ an onion, coarsely chopped

a few sprigs of fresh flat-leaf parsley

a few sprigs of fresh coriander/cilantro

500 g/1 lb. 2 oz. minced/ground lamb

1½ teaspoons sea salt

½ teaspoon ground white pepper

1 teaspoon ground cumin

1 teaspoon paprika

1 tablespoon fresh breadcrumbs (see note on page 26)

4 eggs, to serve (optional)

For the sauce

1½ onions

a small handful of fresh flat-leaf parsley

2 garlic cloves

400-g/14-oz. can chopped tomatoes

300 ml/1¼ cups stock (chicken, lamb or vegetable) or water

1½ teaspoons ground cumin

1 teaspoon ground white pepper

¼ teaspoon ground cinnamon

¼–½ teaspoon cayenne pepper, to taste

a pinch of sugar

Serves 4

To make the meatballs, put the onion in a food processor with the parsley and coriander/cilantro. Process until finely chopped. Add the lamb and process, using the pulse button, to obtain a smooth paste. Transfer to a bowl.

Add the salt, pepper, cumin, paprika and breadcrumbs. Mix well with your hands to combine. Form into walnut-sized balls and transfer to a tray. Cover and set aside.

To make the sauce, put the onions, parsley and garlic in a food processor and process until finely chopped. Transfer to a shallow frying pan/skillet large enough to hold the meatballs in a single layer. Add the tomatoes, stock, cumin, pepper, cinnamon, cayenne and sugar. Stir and bring to the boil, then lower the heat and simmer, covered, for 15 minutes.

Nestle the meatballs in the sauce in a single layer. Cover and simmer for 20–30 minutes, until cooked through.

To serve, divide the meatballs and sauce between shallow soup plates or large bowls, arranging the meatballs in a ring around the perimeter. Poach or lightly fry the eggs if using (keep the yolks runny) and place one cooked egg in the middle of each bowl. Serve immediately.

sausage, pasta and bean stew with greens

Easy to make and even easier to enjoy, this is truly a one-pot meal. It can be served as soon as the sausage and pasta are cooked, which doesn't take long at all, but the taste improves if made in advance. If using spicy sausage, you may not need to add the chilli/hot red pepper flakes. To serve, simply put the pot on the table with a basket of crusty bread and offer extra finely grated Parmesan for sprinkling.

1 tablespoon olive oil

1 large onion, coarsely chopped

12 Italian- or Toulouse-style sausages (about 800 g/1 lb. 12 oz.) cut into bite-sized pieces

4 garlic cloves, sliced

¼–1 teaspoon dried chilli/hot red pepper flakes, to taste

400-g/14-oz. can chopped tomatoes

250 ml/1 cup red wine

1 bay leaf

100 g/generous 1 cup small pasta shapes, such as macaroni

about 175 g/6 oz. greens, such as curly kale, chard or cavolo nero

400-g/14-oz. can cannellini beans, drained

a large handful of fresh basil leaves, chopped

sea salt and freshly ground black pepper

freshly grated Parmesan, to serve

crusty bread, to serve

Serves 4–6

Heat the oil in a large saucepan/pot. Add the onion and cook 3–5 minutes, until soft. Add the sausage and cook for about 5 minutes, until browned. Stir in the garlic and chilli/hot pepper flakes and cook for 1 minute.

Add the tomatoes, wine and bay leaf and enough water to cover. Don't worry if it's soupy at this stage. Bring to the boil, then add the pasta and cook, uncovered, for about 10 minutes, until the pasta is al dente.

Meanwhile bring a separate large saucepan/pot of lightly salted water to the boil. Add the greens and cook briefly just to blanch. Drain and set aside.

Add the blanched greens and beans to the sausage mixture and stir well. Simmer, uncovered, for a further 5 minutes. Taste and adjust the seasoning. Stir in the basil and serve sprinkled with finely grated Parmesan and plenty of crusty bread on the side.

pork stew with sweet potatoes, beans and chilli

The combination of sweet potato and chilli/chile here is fantastic, and it goes well with the melting texture of the pork. Like any stew, this improves with age but is tasty enough to serve the same day it was made. Crusty bread makes a good accompaniment.

Preheat the oven to 150°C (300°F) Gas 2.

Heat 1 tablespoon of the oil in a large flameproof casserole dish. Add the onion and cook for 3–5 minutes, until soft. Stir in 1 teaspoon of the cumin and the oregano and cook for 2–3 minutes, until fragrant. Remove the onion from the casserole dish and set aside.

Add the pork and the remaining tablespoon of oil and cook for 5–7 minutes, until browned all over. Stir in the honey, the remaining cumin, the cinnamon, garlic and chilli/chile. Season with salt and mix well. Return the onions to the pan and add the tomatoes, stock, sweet potatoes and bay leaf. Bring to the boil, then cover and transfer to the preheated oven. Cook for 40 minutes.

Remove from the oven and stir in the beans. Cover and return to the oven to cook for a further 20 minutes. Sprinkle with coriander/cilantro and serve with Greek yoghurt on the side, if liked, and crusty bread.

Vegetarian option: Omit the pork and add 1 diced butternut squash with the sweet potatoes and a 400-g/14-oz. can butter/lima beans with the kidney beans. Replace the chicken stock with vegetable stock. Reduce the cooking time from 40 minutes to 15 minutes.

2 tablespoons olive oil

1 large onion, chopped

2 teaspoons ground cumin

1½ teaspoons dried oregano

700 g/1 lb. 9 oz. pork shoulder, cubed

1 teaspoon runny honey

1 teaspoon ground cinnamon

2 garlic cloves, finely chopped

1 fresh red chilli/chile, deseeded and sliced

400-g/14-oz. can chopped tomatoes

500 ml/2 cups chicken stock

3 sweet potatoes (about 800 g/ 1 lb. 12 oz.), peeled and cubed

1 bay leaf

400-g/14-oz. can kidney beans, drained

a handful of fresh coriander/ cilantro leaves, chopped

sea salt and freshly ground black pepper

Greek yoghurt, to serve (optional)

Serves 4

ham and pasta bake with artichokes, olives and sun-dried tomatoes

This pasta bake is so easy it hardly feels like cooking! It can also be used as a cupboard clearing exercise if lots of jars are stacking up and not getting used. The recipe uses the most common items, but do feel free to experiment with any antipasto-style ingredient that happens to be lurking on your shelves and do not worry if quantities are not exact. Some jars are bigger than others and there is no need to be too precise here.

450 g/7 cups dried pasta shells

125 g/4½ oz.ham or salami, coarsely chopped

295-g/10-oz. jar marinated artichokes, drained and chopped

125 g/1 cup sun-dried tomatoes, drained and chopped

70 g/¾ cup stoned/pitted black olives

2 tablespoons drained capers

4–5 anchovy fillets, coarsely chopped (optional)

500 ml/2 cups any tomato pasta sauce

200 g/generous 1 cup double/ heavy cream, or crème fraîche or sour cream

1 teaspoon dried chilli/hot red pepper flakes (optional)

90 g/3 oz. mild Cheddar or firm mozzarella, grated

3 tablespoons freshly grated Parmesan

sea salt and freshly ground black pepper

a 30 x 20-cm/11¾ x 8-inch baking dish, oiled

Serves 4–6

Preheat the oven to 200°C (400°F) Gas 6.

Cook the pasta according to the packet instructions. Drain well and tip into a large mixing bowl.

Add the ham, artichokes, sun-dried tomatoes, olives, capers and anchovies, if using, to the pasta and mix well.

In a separate bowl or jug/pitcher, stir together the tomato sauce and cream and season lightly. Stir in the chilli/hot red pepper flakes, if using.

Pour the sauce mixture onto the pasta mixture and stir to combine all the ingredients well. Transfer to the prepared baking dish, spread out evenly and level the surface. Sprinkle the top with the grated Cheddar, then finish with the Parmesan.

Bake in the preheated oven for about 20–30 minutes, until the top is golden and bubbling. Serve immediately with a leafy side salad.

mashed potato pie with bacon, leeks and cheese

This is a great way to make a meal out of simple mashed potato. Bacon, leeks and cheese make a particularly perfect trio, but you can add just about anything to this versatile dish. You should have onion at the very least, and cheese of some sort, and something green for a bit of colour, after that anything goes!

1 kg/2 lb. 3 oz. floury potatoes, peeled

2 tablespoons olive oil

1 onion, finely chopped

2 small leeks, thinly sliced

80 g/3 oz. bacon or pancetta, diced

30 g/2 tablespoons butter

250 ml/1 cup milk or single/light cream (or a bit of both)

1 egg, beaten

a large handful of fresh flat-leaf parsley leaves, chopped

a pinch of paprika

90 g/3 oz. firm cheese, such as Gruyère, grated

sea salt and freshly ground black pepper

a 24-cm/9½ x 8-inch round baking dish, well buttered

Serves 4–6

Halve or quarter the potatoes depending on their size; they should be about the same to cook evenly. Put them in a large saucepan/pot, add sufficient cold water to cover, salt well and bring to the boil. Simmer for about 20 minutes, until tender and easily pierced with a skewer.

Meanwhile, heat the oil in a frying pan/skillet set over low heat. Add the onion and leeks and cook gently for about 10 minutes, until soft. Add the bacon and cook for 3–5 minutes, until just browned. Season with salt and set aside.

Preheat the oven to 190°C (375°F) Gas 5.

Drain the potatoes and mash coarsely, mixing in the butter and milk. Season well and add the egg. Stir to combine thoroughly.

Stir in the leek mixture, parsley, paprika and half the cheese. Transfer to the prepared dish and spread evenly. Sprinkle over the remaining cheese and bake in the preheated oven for 35–45 minutes, until well browned. Serve immediately.

chicory gratin with ham and blue cheese

This is a French recipe which traditionally calls for Gruyère cheese only, but the blue cheese used in addition to it here makes it even better. There are many kinds of blue cheese and any firm one will do for this dish. You can also experiment with different kinds of ham; cured ham works especially well. Or, omit the ham altogether for an indulgent vegetarian supper. This is an exceptional way to prepare what is often thought of as a salad-only vegetable. Serve with boiled potatoes or crusty bread and a crisp green salad.

6 chicory/Belgian endive (about 90 g/3 oz. each), rinsed and dried

1–2 tablespoons olive oil

12 slices smoked ham (omit for a vegetarian option)

2–3 tablespoons freshly grated Gruyère or Parmesan

sea salt

For the sauce

50 g/3½ tablespoons unsalted butter

35 g/¼ cup plain/all-purpose flour

600 ml/2½ cups hot milk

½ teaspoon sea salt

½ teaspoon paprika

100 g/3½ oz. grated Gruyère

65 g/2½ oz. any firm blue cheese, crumbled

a 33 x 21-cm/13 x 8¼-inch baking dish, well buttered

Serves 4–6

Preheat the oven to 200°C (400°F) Gas 6.

Halve the chicory/Belgian endive lengthways. Drizzle with the oil and rub with your hands to coat evenly. Arrange in a single layer on a baking sheet. Sprinkle lightly with salt and drizzle over about 4 tablespoons of water. Roast in the preheated oven for about 15 minutes, until just tender when pierced with a knife. Remove from the oven and let cool. Leave the oven on.

Meanwhile, prepare the sauce. Melt the butter in a heavy-based saucepan. Stir in the flour and cook, stirring constantly, for 1 minute. Pour in the hot milk gradually, whisking/beating constantly and continue whisking/beating gently for 3–5 minutes, until the sauce begins to thicken. Season with salt and paprika and add both the cheeses. Stir well to combine.

As soon as the chicory/Belgian endive are cool enough to handle, carefully wrap each one with a slice of ham and arrange them side-by-side, seam-side down, in the prepared baking dish. Pour over the sauce, spreading evenly to coat. Sprinkle with the Gruyère and blue cheese and bake in the hot oven for about 20–30 minutes, until browned and bubbling. Serve immediately with boiled new potatoes or crusty bread and a leafy green salad.

poultry

chicken tarragon bake with orzo

This recipe came into existence for a few reasons. First, chicken and tarragon are a fantastic partnership. But mostly, this is a clever use for leftover roast chicken and the accompanying vegetables, so chicken and vegetable quantities are approximate; a bit more or less is not a problem. Same for the vegetables, and you can use just about anything alongside the carrots or instead of them, green beans, peas, sweetcorn, and so on. If you are making this from scratch, steaming the chicken and carrots together is the easiest option.

350 g/12 oz. cooked chicken, shredded

2 carrots, quartered lengthways, chopped and cooked

200 g/2 cups orzo (see note)

1 tablespoon olive oil

3 tablespoons fresh breadcrumbs (see note on page 26)

sea salt and freshly ground black pepper

For the sauce

50 g/3½ tablespoons butter

35 g/¼ cup plain/all-purpose flour

600 ml/2½ cups hot milk

½ teaspoon sea salt

250 ml/1 cup chicken stock

2 teaspoons wholegrain mustard

2 heaped tablespoons finely chopped fresh tarragon

a 33 x 21-cm/13 x 8¼-inch baking dish, well buttered

Serves 4

Preheat the oven to 200°C (400°F) Gas 6.

First prepare the sauce. Melt the butter in a heavy-based saucepan. Stir in the flour and cook, stirring constantly, for 1 minute. Add the hot milk gradually, whisking/ beating constantly, and continue whisking/beating gently for 3–5 minutes, until the sauce begins to thicken. Stir in the salt, stock, mustard and tarragon and mix to combine. Taste and adjust the seasoning if necessary.

Put the chicken, carrots and orzo in the baking dish. Add the oil, and season with salt if the chicken and vegetables are not already seasoned, and mix. Stir in the sauce and spread evenly in the prepared baking dish. Sprinkle the breadcrumbs over the top. Cover with foil and bake in the preheated oven for 20 minutes, then remove the foil and continue baking for 20–30 minutes, until browned. Serve immediately.

Note: The Italian word orzo means barley although orzo is in fact a type of pasta. When cooked, it has a texture similar to risotto rice. Look for it in the specialist sections of supermarkets, or in Greek, Italian and Middle Eastern delis. It can go by a variety of other names including puntaletti and romarino. If you can't find it, use another small pasta, like trofie.

chicken and spinach gratin with ricotta

A straightforward dish that's sure to be a crowd-pleaser, this is a sort of deconstructed lasagne with chicken instead of minced/ground beef. I tend to use leftover roast chicken for this recipe which makes it quick and easy to prepare.

Put the oil in a large saucepan/pot and set over medium heat. Add the onion and thyme and cook for 3–5 minutes, until soft. Add the garlic, chilli/hot red pepper flakes and parsley and cook for 1 minute. Add the wine and cook for 1 minute. Stir in the passata and sugar and season generously. Reduce the heat and simmer gently, uncovered, for 20–30 minutes.

Meanwhile, cook the pasta tubes according to the packet instructions, drain and set aside until needed.

Preheat the oven to 200°C (400°F) Gas 6.

Stir the ricotta into the tomato sauce until fully blended. Put the chicken, cooked pasta and spinach in the baking dish and toss well to combine. Pour over the sauce, stir well and spread evenly in the dish. Sprinkle the Cheddar and Parmesan over the top.

Bake in the preheated oven for 20–30 minutes, until golden brown. Serve immediately.

1 onion, finely chopped

2 tablespoons olive oil

1 teaspoon dried thyme

3 garlic cloves, sliced

½–1 teaspoon dried chilli/hot red pepper flakes, to taste

a large handful of fresh flat-leaf parsley leaves, chopped

125 ml/½ cup dry white wine

700-g/1½-lb. bottle passata (Italian strained tomatoes)

a pinch of sugar

125 g/1¼ cups dried pasta tubes

250 g/generous 1 cup ricotta

225 g/8 oz. cooked chicken, shredded

200 g/¾ cup frozen leaf spinach, defrosted

100 g/3½ oz. Cheddar, grated

3 tablespoons grated Parmesan

sea salt and freshly ground black pepper

a 25-cm/9¾-inch round baking dish

Serves 4

farmhouse chicken casserole with carrots, leeks and potato

This is the sort of dish I make on Sunday evening to provide a meal or two during the week so I always make a big batch. But you will need a good-sized casserole dish or other lidded flameproof dish, ideally large enough to take the chicken in a single layer.

2–3 tablespoons olive oil

1 small chicken (about 600 g/ 1 lb. 5 oz.), cut into pieces, plus 4 chicken thighs

600 g/1 lb. 5 oz. carrots, peeled and sliced thickly

500 g/1 lb. 2 oz. trimmed leeks, cut into thick rounds

800 g/1 lb. 12 oz. small new potatoes, cut lengthways into wedges

a few sprigs each of fresh thyme and flat-leaf parsley and a bay leaf, tied firmly into a bundle with string

sea salt and freshly ground black pepper

To serve

200 ml/scant 1 cup single/ light cream

2 tablespoons wholegrain Dijon mustard

a large handful of fresh flat-leaf parsley leaves, chopped

a bunch of fresh chives, snipped (optional)

a large flameproof casserole dish

Serves 6–8

Preheat the oven to 150°C (300°F) Gas 2.

Heat 2 tablespoons of the oil in a casserole dish and set over medium heat. Add the chicken pieces, skin-side down, and cook for 4–5 minutes on each side, until browned. Transfer to a dish and season generously with salt. Cover and set aside.

If there is a lot of fat in the casserole dish drain some of it off, leaving just enough to brown the vegetables. Add the carrots and leeks and cook for 5–7 minutes, stirring occasionally, until just brown. Add the potatoes and herb bundle and cook for a further 2–3 minutes. Season with salt.

Return the chicken to the casserole dish and add sufficient water just to cover. Bring to the boil, cover with a lid and transfer to the preheated oven. Cook for about 1 hour.

Return the casserole dish to the hob and uncover. Using a slotted spoon, transfer the chicken and vegetables to a large serving platter. Cook the juices over medium heat for 3–5 minutes to reduce slightly, then stir in the cream. Bring to the boil, then reduce the heat and simmer gently, uncovered, for 5 minutes. Stir in the mustard, parsley and chives and a few grinds of black pepper. Taste for seasoning and adjust as necessary. Pour the sauce over the chicken and vegetables and serve immediately.

chicken tagine with chickpeas and apricots

A tagine may sound exotic but these traditional Moroccan stews are actually very simple to prepare. The dried apricots may seem an unusual addition but they do lend a pleasant sweetness to the spices. This is best served with couscous and a small dish of harissa paste.

2 small chickens, cut into pieces

4 garlic cloves, crushed

1¼ teaspoons ground ginger

1 teaspoon coarsely ground black pepper

1 teaspoon sea salt

2 tablespoons vegetable oil

a large pinch of powdered saffron

1 teaspoon ground cinnamon

1 teaspoon ground turmeric

1 onion, grated

a handful each of chopped fresh flat-leaf parsley and coriander/cilantro leaves

400-g/14-oz. can chickpeas, drained

200 g/1⅓ cups dried stoned/pitted apricots

6 fresh lemon wedges

couscous, to serve

harissa paste, to serve (optional)

a large flameproof casserole dish

Serves 6

Place the chicken in a shallow non-metal dish and add the garlic, ginger, pepper, salt and oil. Toss well to coat. Cover and marinate at room temperatue for at least 30 minutes, or refrigerate overnight.

Transfer the chicken and marinade to a large casserole dish. Add the saffron, cinnamon, turmeric, onion, parsley and coriander/cilantro. Add sufficient water to just cover. Bring to the boil, then reduce the heat, cover with a lid and simmer for 30 minutes.

Add the chickpeas and apricots, stir and adjust the seasoning. Simmer, covered, for a further 20 minutes.

Just before serving garnish each plate with a fresh lemon wedge for squeezing. Serve with couscous and a small dish of harissa paste on the side as a spicy condiment, if liked.

southwestern chicken casserole

A great weeknight supper – healthy and ready in no time. Any chicken pieces can be used, but a packet of chicken thighs in the freezer is a good back up; just remember to defrost them completely before use. Serve with rice and steamed or roasted courgettes/zucchini.

8 chicken thighs, trimmed of any excess skin or fat

1 large onion, chopped

1 green (bell) pepper, chopped

1 tablespoon vegetable oil (optional)

2 garlic cloves, crushed

1 teaspoon ground cumin

1 teaspoon dried oregano

½ teaspoon cayenne pepper

3 fresh plum tomatoes, cored and coarsely chopped

1 tablespoon tomato purée/paste

400 ml/1⅔ cups chicken stock

150 g/1 cup sweetcorn kernels

400-g/14-oz. can kidney beans, drained

2–3 tablespoons drained and chopped pickled jalapeños

a handful of fresh coriander/cilantro leaves, chopped

sea salt and freshly ground black pepper

To serve

fresh lime wedges

4–6 chopped spring onions/scallions

200 g/7 oz. grated mild Cheddar

200 ml/¾ cup sour cream

a large flameproof casserole dish

Serves 4–6

Set a large casserole dish over medium heat. Add the chicken, skin-side down, and cook for 4–5 minutes on each side, until browned. Transfer to a plate and season.

Drain off most of the fat from the casserole dish, add the onion and green (bell) pepper and the oil only if required. Cook for about 3–5 minutes, until golden, scraping the pan to remove any cooked on chicken bits. Stir in the garlic, cumin, oregano, cayenne and a good pinch of salt. Cook, stirring, for 1 minute more.

Add the tomatoes, tomato purée/paste and stock and stir well. Bring to the boil, then return the chicken to the casserole dish. Reduce the heat, cover and simmer for about 30 minutes, until the chicken is cooked through.

Using tongs, transfer the chicken pieces to a plate. Add the sweetcorn, kidney beans, jalapeños and coriander/cilantro to the casserole dish and mix well. Increase the heat and cook, uncovered, for 1–2 minutes, until the sauce has reduced slightly. Taste and adjust the seasoning if necessary. Return the chicken to the casserole dish.

Just before serving, squeeze over the lime juice and serve with bowls of spring onion/scallion, grated cheese and sour cream on the side.

chicken tetrazzini

The origins of this dish are unclear; is it Italian or is it American? Conventional recipes call for sherry, which I never have in my cupboard, but feel free to use some in place of the wine or balsamic vinegar if you do have some; medium dry is best. The peas are also a flourish, added for extra colour and flavour. This dish comes together quickly and will be sure to please all. It is also a good way to use up chicken or even turkey.

350 g/12 oz. wholewheat spaghetti

2–3 tablespoons olive oil

500 g/1 lb. 2 oz. chicken thigh meat, cut into bite-sized pieces

1 small onion, halved and thinly sliced

2 tablespoons dry white wine, balsamic vinegar or sherry

200 g/7 oz. mushrooms, thinly sliced

a large handful of fresh flat-leaf parsley leaves, chopped

75 g/scant ½ cup frozen peas

3–4 tablespoons freshly grated Parmesan

sea salt and freshly ground black pepper

For the sauce

50 g/3½ tablespoons unsalted butter

35 g/¼ cup plain/all-purpose flour

500 ml/2 cups hot chicken stock

100 ml/scant ½ cup double/heavy cream

a 30 x 20 cm/11¾ x 8-inch baking dish, well buttered

Serves 4–6

Preheat the oven to 190°C (375°F) Gas 5.

Cook the spaghetti according to the packet instructions. Drain well and toss in a little olive oil. Set aside.

Heat 1 tablespoon of the oil in a large non-stick frying pan/skillet. Add the chicken and onion and cook for about 5 minutes, stirring occasionally, until browned. Season well, add the wine and cook for a further 3–5 minutes, until the liquid has almost evaporated. Transfer to a plate and set aside.

Heat the remaining 2 tablespoons of oil in the same pan. Add the mushrooms and cook for 3–5 minutes, stirring often, until just soft. Season well and stir in the parsley. Remove from the heat and set aside.

To make the sauce, melt the butter in a heavy-based saucepan set over low heat. Add the flour and cook, stirring, for 1 minute. Slowly pour in the hot stock and cream, whisking/beating continuously, and simmer until the mixture thickens. Season to taste.

Stir in the chicken mixture, the mushrooms and the peas and mix well.

Combine the chicken mixture and cooked spaghetti in a mixing bowl and toss to distribute the ingredients evenly. Transfer to the prepared baking dish and spread evenly. Sprinkle with Parmesan and a generous grating of black pepper. Bake in the preheated oven for 20–30 minutes, until just golden. Serve immediately.

chicken pot pie with tarragon and leeks

True confessions time: I am not confident making pies with pastry bottoms because the crust often comes out soggy. So this is a top-only pie, allowing the herb-infused sauce to shine through without any distractions. A simple mixed salad is the perfect accompaniment and makes this a wholesome family meal that's also suitable when feeding friends.

1 tablespoon olive oil

1 tablespoon butter

1 onion, chopped

2 carrots, sliced

2 trimmed leeks, sliced

a splash of dry white wine (optional)

60 g/1 cup button mushrooms, quartered

500 g/1 lb. 2 oz. cooked chicken, cut into bite-sized pieces

75 g/scant ½ cup frozen peas

375 g/13 oz. ready-rolled puff pastry, defrosted if frozen

a little beaten egg, for glazing

sea salt and freshly ground black pepper

For the sauce

50 g/3½ tablespoons butter

35 g/¼ cup plain/all-purpose flour

500 ml/2 cups hot chicken stock

100 ml/scant ½ cup single/light cream

several sprigs of fresh tarragon, leaves stripped and chopped

a bunch of fresh chives, snipped

leaves from a small bunch of fresh parsley, finely chopped

a 30 x 20 cm/11¾ x 8-inch baking dish

Serves 4–6

Preheat the oven to 190°C (375°F) Gas 5.

Heat the oil and butter in a large non-stick frying pan/skillet. Add the onion, carrots and leeks and cook, stirring occasionally, for 5–8 minutes, until soft. Season well with salt and pepper, add the mushrooms and wine, if using, and cook for 3–5 minutes more. You may need to add a drop more oil or butter. Add the chicken and peas, and set aside.

To make the sauce, melt the butter in a heavy-based saucepan set over low heat. Add the flour and cook for 1 minute, stirring continuously. Slowly pour in the hot stock and cream, whisking/beating continuously, and simmer until the mixture thickens. Season well. Stir in the tarragon, chives and parsley. Taste and adjust the seasoning if necessary.

Transfer the chicken mixture to the baking dish and pour over the sauce. Mix to combine.

Unroll the pastry on a lightly floured surface. Lay the sheet on top of the filling, crimping the edges to sit just inside the edge and trimming off any excess with a sharp knife (you can use the trimmings for decoration, if liked). Cut an 'X' in the middle to allow steam to escape and brush with the beaten egg. Bake in the preheated oven for 30–40 minutes, until golden brown. Serve immediately.

Vegetarian option: Omit the chicken and use vegetable stock. Increase the carrot, leek and mushroom quantities slightly and add 300 g/10½ oz. of any one or a combination of the following vegetables which has been cooked and cubed where appropriate: swede/rutabaga, parsnip, broccoli and/or cauliflower florets, courgettes/zucchini, green beans or asparagus.

braised duck and white bean cassoulet

The idea of long-simmered duck in a garlicky sauce is always appetizing, but not always easy to achieve due to time constraints. This is shortcut cassoulet, but cassoulet in spirit because it combines duck with smoked bacon and a browned topping of white beans. It's a good dish for cold weather and easy to prepare in advance. Simply add a mixed green salad and crusty bread for a substantial and satisfying meal that's great for entertaining.

4 duck legs (about 400 g/
14 oz. each)

2 onions, halved and sliced

1 large carrot, diced

150 g/5½ oz. pancetta or
lardons, diced

1 teaspoon dried thyme

4 garlic cloves, sliced

250 ml/1 cup dry white wine

2 x 400-g/14-oz. cans chopped
tomatoes

125 g/1 cup stoned/pitted
green olives

1 bay leaf

2 x 400-g/14-oz. cans haricot
or cannellini beans, drained

about 100 g/1¼ cups
breadcrumbs (see note on
page 26)

sea salt and freshly ground
black pepper

*a 33 x 21-cm/13 x 8¼-inch
baking dish*

Serves 4–6

Preheat the oven to 170°C (325°F) Gas 3.

Arrange the duck legs skin-side down in a large saucepan/ pot and cook over medium heat for 4–5 minutes on each side, until browned. Transfer to a plate and sprinkle with salt.

Drain off all but 1 tablespoon of fat from the pan. Add the onions and carrots and cook for about 5 minutes, until soft. Add the pancetta and thyme and cook for a further 3–4 minutes. Add the garlic and cook for 1 minute. Season and add the wine. Bring to the boil and boil, uncovered, for 1 minute. Add the tomatoes, olives and bay leaf. Reduce the heat and simmer, uncovered, for 5 minutes. Taste and adjust the seasoning if necessary.

Using tongs, transfer the duck legs to the baking dish. Pour over the sauce and spread evenly. If necessary, add sufficient water to submerge the duck by about 2.5 cm/1 inch. Cover tightly with foil and transfer to the preheated oven to cook for 1½ hours. Check after 1 hour. (The recipe can be prepared up to 24 hours in advance up to this point. Cover and refrigerate until needed.)

Remove the baking dish from the oven and increase the heat to 200°C (400°F) Gas 6.

Add the beans to the dish in an even layer, sprinkle the breadcrumbs over the top and season well. Return to the oven and bake for 20–25 minutes more, until well browned on top. Serve immediately.

chicken and sweet potato pie

Americans tend to eat sweet potatoes and bread stuffing as part of the holiday season festivities. This recipe is designed to enjoy at any time. It is also designed as a way to recycle leftover roast chicken but you could be forgiven for buying a supermarket rotisserie chicken expressly for this dish. To obtain the stale bread, I use the end pieces from sliced loaves that never seem to get eaten, and toast them in the oven, alongside the sweet potatoes. This is a meal in a single dish, requiring only a green salad and good appetites.

1.5 kg/2 lb. 11 oz. sweet potatoes, peeled and cut into chunks

3–4 tablespoons olive oil

2–4 tablespoons butter

1 onion, diced

100 g/3½ oz. bacon, chopped

150 g/5½ oz. mushrooms, chopped

2 celery sticks/stalks, chopped

2 garlic cloves, crushed

2 teaspoons dried thyme

75–100 g/2½–3½ oz. sausages, cooked and chopped

100 g/¾ cup vacuum-packed peeled chestnuts, chopped

a large handful of fresh flat-leaf parsley leaves, chopped

½ a chicken (about 700 g/9 oz.), cooked and meat shredded

125 g/4½ oz. stale or toasted bread, broken into small pieces

5 tablespoons milk

180 ml/¾ cup chicken stock or water

sea salt and freshly ground black pepper

a 25–30-cm/9¾–11¾-inch round baking dish, well buttered

Serves 4–6

Preheat the oven to 220°C (425°F) Gas 7.

Toss the sweet potatoes with the olive oil and arrange in a single layer on a baking sheet. Roast in the preheated oven for about 45 minutes, until tender and browned. Reduce the oven temperature to 200°C (400°F) Gas 6. Let the sweet potatoes cool, then peel, mash with butter to taste and season with salt. Set aside.

Heat some of the oil in a frying pan/skillet. Add the onion and cook for 2–3 minutes, until soft. Season with salt, then add the bacon, mushrooms and celery and cook for 3–5 minutes, stirring often. Add the garlic, thyme, sausage and chestnuts and cook for about 1 minute. Stir in the parsley and chicken and set aside.

In a bowl, combine the bread pieces and milk and toss to coat. The bread should be moist, you may need to add more milk. Add the bread to the chicken mixture, along with the stock. Stir well. Taste and adjust the seasoning.

Spread the chicken mixture in an even layer in the prepared baking dish. It will dry out slightly with baking, so if it seems dry at the outset, add a bit more of any liquid: stock, milk or water. Top with the mashed sweet potato, spread evenly. Bake in the preheated oven for about 45 minutes. (The sweet potato won't brown but should start to blacken slightly where peaked.)

chicken meatballs with roasted onions and tomatoes

Not your average meatball, these rarely come out perfectly round but their imperfection is part of their charm. An unusual meatball requires something more exotic than just tomato sauce, hence the roasted tomatoes and onions, which works a treat. Serve with mash.

Preheat the oven to 200°C (400°F) Gas 6.

Halve 1 of the onions and chop coarsely; set aside. Cut the remaining onions into quarters and toss with 2–3 tablespoons of the oil and the thyme. Arrange on the foil-lined baking sheet with the tomatoes. Set aside while you prepare the meatballs.

In a small food processor combine the coarsely chopped onion, mushrooms, pancetta and parsley. Process until finely chopped. Transfer to a frying pan/skillet and add 1–2 tablespoons of the oil. Cook for 3–5 minutes, until softened. Add the garlic, season well and cook for 1 minute more. Let cool slightly.

In a bowl, combine the chicken, paprika, egg, breadcrumbs and the cooled mushroom mixture. Add a good pinch of salt. Mix well with your hands to combine. Take a small pinch of the mixture and cook it in the pan used to cook the mushroom mixture. When cooked, taste it and adjust the seasoning as necessary. The mixture should be quite moist and it will be possible – if difficult – to form the mixture into balls. If it is too dry, soften with milk, adding 1 tablespoon at a time.

Form the chicken mixture into roughly shaped meatballs, about the size of a large walnut, and arrange them on the paper-lined baking sheet. Season the onions and tomatoes and put both of the sheets into the preheated oven. Bake for about 35–45 minutes, until the meatballs and vegetables are browned. Serve together.

Note: If you have space, 2 sheets can fit alongside one another in extra wide ovens. But do not place 1 sheet on a shelf above the other as the contents of the bottom sheet will not brown properly. If this is a problem, best to roast the vegetables first, then set aside while roasting the meatballs and reheat just before serving.

3 onions

6 fresh plum tomatoes, cored and quartered

4 tablespoons olive oil

1 teaspoon dried thyme

125 g/4½ oz. mushrooms, coarsely chopped

100 g/3½ oz. pancetta or ham

a large handful of fresh flat-leaf parsley leaves, chopped

2 garlic cloves, crushed

500 g/1 lb. 2 oz. minced/ ground chicken

1 teaspoon paprika

1 egg, beaten

5 tablespoons fresh breadcrumbs (see note on page 26)

milk, to soften

sea salt and freshly ground black pepper

2 baking sheets, 1 lined with foil the other with baking parchment

Serves 4–6

Spanish-style chicken and rice

This is really a cheat's paella, but it tastes just as good as the real thing. The shortcut here is the oven baking; easier than stirring and watching over the stovetop like a hawk. It's a meal in itself, but a nice bottle of Spanish red and some crusty bread would not go amiss.

1 tablespoon olive oil

8 chicken thighs, trimmed of excess skin and fat

1 onion, diced

1 orange or yellow (bell) pepper, deseeded and diced

1 carrot, peeled and diced

4 garlic cloves, crushed

½ teaspoon Spanish smoked sweet paprika (pimentón dulce)

380 g/generous 2 cups paella rice

6–8 cooking chorizo (about 250 g/9 oz.), cut into large pieces

125 ml/½ cup dry white wine

300 ml/1¼ cups chicken stock

400-g/14-oz. can chopped tomatoes

1 bay leaf

200 g/1⅔ cups frozen peas

a handful of fresh flat-leaf parsley leaves, chopped

sea salt and freshly ground black pepper

a large flameproof casserole dish

Serves 4

Preheat the oven to 200°C (400°F) Gas 6.

Heat the oil in a casserole dish. Add the chicken, skin-side down, and cook for 3–5 minutes on each side, until browned. Transfer to a plate and season with salt.

Add the onion, (bell) pepper and carrot to the casserole dish and cook for 2–3 minutes. Add the garlic, paprika, rice and chorizo and continue cooking, stirring to coat the rice in oil, for about 1 minute more.

Stir in the wine, stock and tomatoes, add the bay leaf and season well. Return the chicken to the casserole dish. Cover with a lid and transfer to the preheated oven. Cook for 20 minutes. Remove the casserole dish from the oven and stir in the peas. Return to the oven and cook for a further 10 minutes, until the rice is tender. (If it seems dry when adding the peas, add a splash of water.)

Remove from the oven and let stand, covered, for about 10 minutes. Remove the bay leaf, stir in the parsley, fluff up the rice with a fork and serve.

Moroccan chicken filo pie

Ideal for large gatherings or buffets, this is best when made in advance giving the flavours time to mingle. The filling can also be made into individual pies or pastries. Serve with a grated carrot salad dressed with orange juice and olive oil, and couscous with chickpeas.

2 tablespoons olive oil

1 onion, grated

1 teaspoon ground cinnamon

2 teaspoons ground ginger

½ teaspoon turmeric

a pinch of saffron threads

1 teaspoon paprika

½ teaspoon ground cumin

½ teaspoon ground black pepper

1 garlic clove, crushed

8 chicken thighs, skin removed

40 g/¼ cup raisins

35 g/½ cup flaked/slivered almonds

a large handful of fresh coriander/cilantro leaves, chopped

1 tablespoon freshly squeezed lemon juice

270 g/9½ oz. filo/phyllo pastry

2–3 tablespoons butter, melted

sea salt and freshly ground black pepper

a 24-cm/9½-inch round baking dish or tart pan, well buttered

Serves 4–6

Heat the oil in a large saucepan/pot set over low heat. Add the onion and cook for 5–8 minutes, until just soft. Stir in the spices and garlic and cook for 1 minute. Add the chicken and stir to coat in the spiced oil. Add 190 ml/ ¾ cup water and the raisins. Season generously with salt. Bring to the boil, reduce the heat, cover and simmer for about 20–30 minutes, until the chicken is cooked through. Set aside.

Preheat the oven to 190°C (375°F) Gas 5.

When the chicken is cool enough to handle, shred the meat and discard the bones. Return the meat to the cooking juices. Mix well, taste and adjust the seasoning. The mixture should be very moist but it should not be soupy. If there is a lot of liquid, return to the heat and cook to reduce slightly. Stir in the almonds, coriander/ cilantro and lemon juice. Set aside.

To assemble, place 2 sheets of filo/phyllo on the work surface. Using the baking dish as a template, cut out 2 circles of pastry to fit. Cover with a clean, damp kitchen towel/dish cloth and set aside. Line the sides of the dish with the remaining pastry sheets, positioning each one with an overhang and not quite reaching the middle. Continue until the edge is covered with overhanging sheets of pastry. Brush the bottom of the dish with melted butter and top with one of the pastry circles. Brush with more butter and top with the remaining circle.

Transfer the chicken mixture to the filo/phyllo-lined dish, spreading it evenly. Fold in the overhanging pastry to part-enclose the filling, crinkling it as you go. Brush with melted butter. Bake in the preheated oven for 30–40 minutes, until just golden. Serve warm or at room temperature.

ginger and star anise braised chicken

A wonderfully simple and healthy way to enjoy chicken that will also fill your kitchen with exotic aromas. This is a real crowd-pleaser and it gets better over time so it is worthwhile preparing it in advance, or making a big batch to ensure leftovers. To do this, use two small chickens, or 1 medium and a packet of chicken pieces, such as thighs, and double all the other ingredients. Serve with boiled rice and accompany with steamed or sautéed mangetout/snow peas.

1 tablespoon vegetable oil

1 medium chicken (800–900 g/
1 lb. 12 oz.–2 lb.), cut into
serving pieces

15-g/½-oz. piece of fresh ginger,
peeled and cut into thin strips

3 garlic cloves, sliced

80 ml/⅓ cup Chinese rice wine

125 ml/½ cup chicken stock
or water

1 tablespoon runny honey

1 star anise

60 ml/¼ cup light soy sauce

freshly squeezed juice of
1 clementine (or 3–4 tablespoons
fresh orange juice)

2 spring onions/scallions,
thinly sliced on the diagonal

boiled rice, to serve

sea salt

Serves 4

Heat the oil in a large saucepan/pot. When hot, add the chicken pieces, skin-side down, and cook for about 4–5 minutes on each side, until browned. Transfer to a plate, season lightly with salt and set aside.

Drain all but 1 tablespoon of fat from the pan. Add the ginger, garlic, rice wine, stock, honey, star anise and soy sauce and bring to the boil. Add the clementine juice and the chicken. Reduce the heat, cover and simmer gently for 15 minutes. Turn the chicken pieces and simmer for about 15 minutes more, until cooked through. Taste and adjust the seasoning if necessary.

Remove the chicken from the pan with a slotted spoon and set aside. Bring the liquid back to the boil and cook for 2–3 minutes to reduce slightly. Remove the star anise, return the chicken the pan and stir to coat in the sauce. Sprinkle with spring onions/scallions and serve with boiled rice and mangetout/snow peas, if liked.

spicy chicken casserole with sweet peppers

Colourful with fantastic flavours, this recipe is one I return to time and time again.
The (bell) pepper mixture is inspired by a traditional French Basque country recipe
for piperade, which is usually made to accompany grilled tuna steaks and sometimes
scrambled eggs. Rice makes a good accompaniment, as does a simple green salad.

2 tablespoons olive oil

1 large chicken (about 2 kg/
4 lb. 8 oz.), cut into 8 pieces

2 onions halved and sliced

2 red (bell) peppers, halved,
deseeded and sliced

2 yellow (bell) peppers, halved,
deseeded and sliced

4 garlic cloves, crushed

2 fresh green chillies/chiles,
thinly sliced

¼ teaspoon cayenne pepper
(optional)

125 ml/½ cup dry white wine

400-g/14-oz. can chopped
tomatoes

a large handful of fresh flat-leaf
parsley leaves, chopped

a pinch of sugar

sea salt and freshly ground
black pepper

boiled rice, to serve

Serves 4

Heat the oil in a large frying pan/skillet set over medium
heat. Add the chicken pieces skin-side down and cook for
5–10 minutes on each side, until browned. Transfer the
chicken to a plate, season with salt and set aside.

Add the onions and (bell) peppers to the pan, season and
cook for 10–15 minutes, stirring occasionally, until soft.
Stir in the garlic and chilli/chile and cook for 1 minute.
If you want this really hot, add the cayenne. Add the wine
and cook for 3–5 minutes, until most of the liquid has
reduced. Stir in the tomatoes, parsley and sugar. Taste
and adjust the seasoning as necessary. Return the chicken
to the pan and bury it in the sauce.

Reduce the heat, cover and simmer for 30–40 minutes,
until the chicken is tender and cooked through. Serve
immediately with boiled rice.

coconut chicken curry with spiced lentil dhal and potatoes

3 tablespoons vegetable oil

450 g/1 lb. boneless chicken, cut into pieces

3 tablespoons garam masala

200 ml/¾ cup coconut milk

3 tablespoons cumin seeds

2 tablespoons black mustard seeds

1 onion, very finely chopped

25-g/¾-oz. piece of fresh ginger, peeled and grated (about 1 tablespoon)

3 garlic cloves, crushed

1 fresh red chilli/chile, chopped

3 teaspoons ground cumin

1 teaspoon ground turmeric

¼–1 teaspoon cayenne pepper, to taste

1 tablespoon tomato purée/paste

500 ml/2 cups chicken or vegetable stock

1 cinnamon stick

250 g/1½ cups split red lentils

350 g/12 oz. new potatoes, scrubbed or peeled and cubed

150 g/scant 1½ cups frozen peas

1 tablespoon runny honey

freshly squeezed juice of 1 lemon

sea salt

a handful of fresh coriander/cilantro leaves, to serve

warmed naan bread, to serve

Serves 6–8

This is a long list of ingredients, but the dish comes together very quickly so don't let it put you off. As with most highly spiced dishes, this benefits from being made in advance, to allow the spices time to mingle, but it's still delicious enough to stand up to a last minute whim for immediate consumption. Serve with warmed naan bread.

Heat 1 tablespoon of the oil in a large frying pan/skillet set over medium heat. Add the chicken and 2 tablespoons of the garam masala and season well with salt. Cook for 3–5 minutes, stirring, until golden. Add the coconut milk and simmer for about 10 minutes, until the chicken is cooked. Set aside.

Heat the remaining oil in a large saucepan/pot. Add the cumin and mustard seeds, and cook until they begin to pop. Stir in the onion, ginger, garlic, chilli/chile, cumin, turmeric, cayenne, tomato purée/paste and remaining garam masala and cook, stirring, for 1–2 minutes.

Add the stock, 200 ml/¾ cup water, cinnamon, lentils and potatoes and mix well. Reduce the heat and simmer, uncovered, for 35–45 minutes, until the potatoes are tender. Check often and top up with water if required; the mixture should be liquid but not overly soupy. Taste and adjust the seasoning if necessary. Stir in the honey and lemon juice.

Stir the chicken mixture into the lentil mixture. Add the peas and simmer for 5 minutes more. Sprinkle with some coriander/cilantro and serve with warmed naan bread.

Vegetarian option: Use vegetable stock and replace the chicken with 500 g/1 lb. 2 oz. blanched cauliflower florets, and simmer in the coconut milk until tender, before adding to the lentils.

fish and shellfish

smoked haddock and potato gratin

This may sound and look rustic but the taste is very sophisticated, making it an ideal choice for when you need to cook something elegant yet easy. Use good-quality undyed smoked haddock fillet for this dish – smoked trout or smoked Alaskan sable are suitable substitutes if haddock is unavailable. Serve the gratin with sautéed fine green beans or, if you are serving it as a midweek supper, then a simple green salad alongside is all that's required.

1.5 kg/3¼ lb. waxy potatoes, peeled

1 bay leaf

15 g/½ oz. dried wild mushrooms

1 onion, chopped

2 tablespoons olive oil

150 g/5½ oz. white mushrooms, sliced

125 ml/½ cup dry white wine

280 g/10 oz. undyed smoked haddock fillet, shredded, bones removed

a large handful of fresh flat-leaf parsley leaves, chopped

265 ml/1 cup plus 1 tablespoon single/light cream

250 ml/1 cup milk

2 tablespoons butter, melted

sea salt and freshly ground black pepper

a 33 x 21-cm/13 x 8¼-inch oval baking dish, well buttered

Serves 4–6

Put the potatoes in a large saucepan/pot, add the bay leaf and add sufficient cold water to cover well. Parboil until almost tender when pierced with a knife. Drain. When cool enough to handle slice into ½-cm/¼-inch thick rounds.

Put the dried mushrooms in a heatproof bowl and add sufficient boiling water to cover. Soak for about 15 minutes, until soft. Discard all but 2 tablespoons of the soaking liquid. Drain the mushrooms, chop coarsely and set aside.

Preheat the oven to 200°C (400°F) Gas 6.

Put 1 tablespoon of the oil in a large frying pan/skillet and add the onion. Cook for 3–5 minutes, until soft. Add the white mushrooms and the remaining oil and season well. Cook, stirring, for 3–5 minutes, until the mushrooms begin to brown. Add the wine and reserved mushroom soaking liquid and cook for 1 minute. Stir in the dried mushrooms, haddock and parsley and cook for 2–3 minutes.

Combine the cream and milk in a bowl or jug/pitcher, season and set aside.

To assemble, arrange half the potato slices on the bottom of the prepared dish (save the most even and attractive slices for the top layer). Sprinkle lightly with salt. Spread the fish mixture in an even layer on top of the potatoes. Top with the remaining potatoes, arranged neatly. Sprinkle lightly with salt, then pour over the cream mixture. Brush the top with melted butter and bake in the preheated oven for about 1–1½ hours, until golden. Serve immediately.

crispy-crumbed fish bake
with mushrooms and tomato

Easy, healthy and full of flavour, this recipe will put a nutritious meal on the table in under an hour. Because there is very little sauce, this goes well with spinach tagliatelle tossed in a bit of cream but it can just as easily be served with plain boiled rice. Accompany with any green side vegetable, such as broccoli or green beans.

50 g/1 cup fresh breadcrumbs (see note on page 26)

½ teaspoon paprika

1 heaped tablespoon finely grated mature/sharp Cheddar

600 g/21 oz. boneless, skinless fish fillets, such as hake or pollock, cut into bite-sized pieces

4 fresh plum tomatoes, cored and very thinly sliced

300 g/2 cups button mushrooms, trimmed and thinly sliced

3 tablespoons dry white wine

3–4 tablespoons butter, cut into small pieces

leaves from a small bunch of fresh flat-leaf parsley, chopped

sea salt and freshly ground black pepper

a 33 x 21 cm/13 x 8¼-inch baking dish, very well buttered

Serves 4

Preheat the oven to 190°C (375°F) Gas 5.

In a small bowl, mix the breadcrumbs with the paprika and season well. Mix in the cheese. Set aside.

Arrange the fish in the prepared baking dish and season well. Arrange an even layer of tomato slices on top and sprinkle lightly with salt. Top with an even layer of mushroom slices. Pour over the wine. Dot the top with butter and sprinkle over the parsley. Sprinkle over the seasoned breadcrumbs in an even layer.

Bake in the preheated oven for 30–40 minutes, until browned and the fish is cooked through. Check after 20 minutes; if the top browns too quickly, cover loosely with foil and continue cooking.

After about 30 minutes cooking time, remove the foil (if using), increase the heat to 220°C (425°F) Gas 7 and cook for 3–5 minutes more, just to crisp and brown the top nicely. Serve immediately.

fish pie with leeks and herbs

A classic British dish, made slightly more stylish here by the addition of leeks and fresh herbs. It is important to use a mixture of different fish, as this gives the dish a more interesting taste and texture, but if smoked fish is difficult to obtain, simply increase the quantity of the others. Serve with peas or wilted fresh spinach.

Put the potatoes in a large saucepan/pot and add sufficient cold water to cover. Add 1 of the bay leaves, season with salt and bring to the boil. Cook until the potatoes are tender when pierced with a knife. Drain well. Working in batches, mash the potatoes with all but 50 g/3½ tablespoons of the butter, 250 ml/1 cup of the milk (warmed) and some salt. Repeat until all the potatoes are mashed. Taste and adjust the seasoning. It should be slightly thinner than ordinary mash to allow for baking. Set aside.

Preheat the oven to 190°C (375°F) Gas 5.

Put the oil in a small saucepan and add the leek. Cook for about 5 minutes, until soft. Season lightly, add the wine and cook until the liquid is almost fully reduced. Set aside.

Add the remaining milk and bay leaf to a large shallow pan and bring to the boil. Add the white fish fillets and poach for about 5 minutes, until almost cooked. Transfer to a plate with a slotted spoon and season. Add the salmon and repeat. Add the smoked haddock and repeat. Transfer the poaching milk to a measuring jug/pitcher; if it is not 600 ml/2½ cups, top it up with more milk.

Melt the remaining butter in a medium saucepan set over low heat. Add the flour and cook, whisking/beating, for 1 minute. Slowly pour in the reserved milk, whisking/beating continuously, and simmer until the mixture thickens. Add the mustard and season to taste. Stir in the chives and parsley.

Break the fish into pieces and put in the prepared dish. Add the prawns/shrimp and leeks. Pour over the sauce and stir to mix. Spread evenly. Top with the mash and spread in an even layer.

Bake in the preheated oven for 35–45 minutes, until browned and bubbling up around the edges. Serve immediately.

1 kg/35 oz. floury potatoes, peeled

2 bay leaves

115 g/1 stick unsalted butter

about 850 ml/3½ cups milk

1 tablespoon olive oil

1 leek, cut into thin rounds

2 tablespoons dry white wine

300 g/10½ oz. cod fillet

200 g/7 oz. boneless, skinless salmon

150 g/5½ oz. smoked haddock

175 g/6 oz. peeled cooked prawns/shrimp

35 g/¼ cup plain/all-purpose flour

1 teaspoon dry mustard powder

a small bunch of chives, snipped

freshly chopped flat-leaf parsley

sea salt and freshly ground black pepper

a 30 x 20 cm/11¾ x 8-inch baking dish, well buttered

Serves 6

fish in veracruz sauce

A feisty, fiery sauce that is a cinch to prepare. This recipe can doubled easily for a crowd, or halved for two. Serve with rice, warmed flour tortillas and avocado slices. This recipe works equally well with other seafood, such as scallops or peeled large prawns/jumbo shrimp.

4 fish fillets (total weight about 750–900 g/26–31 oz.), such as sea bass, hake or red snapper

freshly squeezed juice of 2 limes

3 tablespoons olive oil

1 large onion, finely chopped

4 garlic cloves, crushed

2 x 400-g/14-oz. cans chopped tomatoes

80 g stoned/pitted green olives, sliced

2 tablespoons drained capers (optional)

2–3 tablespoons sliced pickled jalapeños with their juice

3 tablespoons finely chopped fresh flat-leaf parsley leaves

½ teaspoon dried oregano

2 bay leaves

a large handful of fresh coriander/cilantro leaves, chopped

sea salt and freshly ground black pepper

To serve

rice

warmed flour tortillas

2 ripe avocados, stoned/pitted and sliced

lime wedges

Serves 4

Put the fish in a non-reactive dish and pour over the lime juice. Sprinkle with salt, turn with your hands to coat, then cover and marinate while you prepare the sauce. (You can also prepare the fish up to several hours in advance, keep in the refrigerator until needed.)

Heat the oil in a frying pan/skillet large enough to hold all the fish in a single layer. Add the onion and cook over low heat for 5–10 minutes, until soft. Season with salt, add the garlic and cook for 1 minute more.

Add the tomatoes, olives, capers (if using), jalapeños, parsley, oregano and bay leaves. Season, stir to mix and simmer gently for 15 minutes. Taste and adjust the seasoning if necessary.

Add the fish to the pan along with the lime juice marinade, burying the fillets in the sauce. Cover and cook for 3–5 minutes. Turn and continue cooking for 3–5 minutes more, until the fish is opaque and cooked through. Discard the bay leaves and serve immediately with rice, warmed tortillas and slices of avocado.

tuna pasta puttanesca

This dish comes together quickly but always tastes better the next day so make it ahead of time if you can, or make extra to enjoy as leftovers. This is best served with a crisp green salad, crusty bread and a bottle of hearty Italian red wine.

2 tablespoons olive oil

1 onion, finely chopped

1 teaspoon dried oregano

4 garlic cloves, sliced

a large handful of fresh flat-leaf parsley leaves, chopped

½–1 teaspoon dried chilli/ hot red pepper flakes, to taste

125 ml/½ cup dry white or red wine

700-g/1½-lb. jar passata (Italian strained tomatoes)

a pinch of sugar

300 g/4½ cups dried fusilli

80 g/¾ cup stoned/pitted black olives, sliced

1 tablespoon drained capers

4 anchovy fillets in oil, chopped

350-g/12-oz. can tuna in oil, drained and flaked

2–3 tablespoons freshly grated Parmesan

sea salt and freshly ground black pepper

a 33 x 21-cm/13 x 8¼-inch baking dish

Serves 4

Heat the oil in a large saucepan/pot set over medium heat and add the onion and oregano. Cook for 3–5 minutes, stirring, until soft. Add the garlic, parsley and chilli/ hot red pepper flakes and cook for 1 minute. Add the wine and cook for 1 minute. Stir in the passata and sugar and season well. Reduce the heat and simmer gently, uncovered, for 20–30 minutes.

Meanwhile, cook the pasta according to the package instructions. Once cooked, drain, toss in a little oil and set aside.

Preheat the oven to 200°C (400°F) Gas 6.

Stir the olives, capers, anchovies and tuna into the sauce. Taste and adjust the seasoning if necessary. Add the cooked pasta and stir well to combine.

Transfer to a baking dish and spread evenly. Sprinkle the Parmesan over the top and bake in the preheated oven for 20–30 minutes, until golden. Serve immediately.

Burmese fish curry

This is a quick and zesty curry, made fragrant with tomatoes and ginger, which offers a welcome change from the creamy coconut variety. Make this as spicy as you like by adjusting the chilli/chile quantity. It tastes best when assembled at the last minute to keep it fresh, and it also works well with prawns/shrimp and mussels. Serve with basmati rice.

1 large onion, coarsely chopped

2 tablespoons vegetable oil

¼–½ teaspoon dried chilli/hot red pepper flakes

4 garlic cloves, crushed

3 fresh plum tomatoes, cored and chopped

30-g/1-oz. piece of fresh ginger, peeled and grated

1 teaspoon paprika

½ teaspoon ground turmeric

500 g/18 oz. white fish fillets, such as hake or pollock, cut into bite-sized pieces

1–2 fresh green chillies/chiles, diced

1–2 tablespoons Thai fish sauce

a large handful of fresh coriander/cilantro leaves, chopped

sea salt

basmati rice, to serve

4 lemon wedges, to serve

Serves 4

Put the onions in a small food processor and blend until very finely chopped. Heat the oil in a large, deep-sided frying pan/skillet set over low heat. Add the chopped onion and cook for 3–5 minutes, until just soft. Add the chilli/hot red pepper flakes, garlic, tomatoes, ginger, paprika, turmeric and a little salt. Simmer uncovered for 5 minutes, stirring often.

Add the fish, chillies/chiles and 1 tablespoon of the fish sauce to the pan. Add sufficient water to obtain a liquid sauce; it should be thick and soupy.

Cover and cook over low heat for 7–8 minutes, until the fish is cooked through. Taste and add more fish sauce if required. Sprinkle over the coriander/cilantro just before serving. Spoon over rice and offer the lemon wedge on the side for squeezing.

Moroccan fish tagine

This recipe uses an ordinary baking dish, with foil in place of the conical tagine lid. Not authentic, but an acceptable replacement. Another slight modification is the use of fish fillets because it is more traditional to use whole fish, such as sea bass. But the herbs and spices are based on a traditional Moroccan recipe and the taste is fabulously genuine. Serve with couscous or rice, as preferred.

1 kg/35 oz. boneless, skinless white fish fillet

1 onion, coarsely chopped

a handful of fresh flat-leaf parsley leaves

2 garlic cloves, crushed

400-g/14-oz. can chopped tomatoes

4 thin carrots, halved and sliced

1 teaspoon ground cumin

½ teaspoon cayenne pepper

a pinch of sugar

sea salt and freshly ground black pepper

lemon wedges, to serve

couscous or rice, to serve

For the marinade

a small bunch of fresh coriander/cilantro leaves

1 tablespoon coarse sea salt

4 garlic cloves, crushed

2 tablespoons paprika

½ teaspoon cayenne pepper

1 tablespoon ground cumin

freshly squeezed juice of ½ a lemon

125 ml/½ cup olive oil

a shallow baking dish

Serves 4

To make the marinade, combine 2 tablespoons of freshly chopped coriander/cilantro leaves with the salt, garlic, paprika, cayenne, cumin, lemon juice and olive oil in a shallow baking dish (not metal) large enough to hold the fish in a single layer. Mix well. Add the fish, and use your hands to turn the pieces until they are coated in the oil. Cover with clingfilm/plastic wrap and refrigerate while you prepare the sauce (at least 30 minutes and up to several hours).

Preheat the oven to 190°C (375°F) Gas 5.

To make the sauce, put the onion, parsley and garlic in a food processor and process until finely chopped. Transfer to a saucepan set over medium heat. Add the tomatoes, 300 ml/1¼ cups water, carrots, cumin, cayenne and sugar. Season and stir to blend. Bring to the boil, then reduce the heat and simmer, covered, for about 15 minutes, until the carrots are tender.

Remove the fish from the refrigerator. Transfer it to a plate and pour the tomato sauce into the ovenproof dish containing the marinade and mix well. Return the fish to the dish, arranging it on top of the sauce. Cover with foil and bake in the preheated oven for 10–20 minutes, until the fish is cooked through.

Remove from the oven. Grind over some black pepper and garnish with a few coriander/cilantro sprigs. Serve with the lemon wedges for squeezing and couscous or rice, as preferred.

roasted Provençal salmon and vegetables with rouille

Bright and festive, the colours and aromas in this dish will instantly transport you to the south of France. Be sure to choose a wrinkly, gutsy black olive for this dish; ordinary black olives simply won't do. This is ideal for both informal dining or entertaining and in either case you can serve it straight from the sheet pan. Accompany with crusty bread and a green salad lightly dressed with extra virgin olive oil, good quality wine vinegar and lots of fresh herbs.

500 g/18 oz. baby new potatoes, scrubbed and quartered

500 g/18 oz. courgettes/ zucchini, halved and quartered

1 fennel bulb, halved and sliced

1 red (bell) pepper, cored, deseeded and sliced

1 yellow (bell) pepper, cored, deseeded and sliced

3 fresh plum tomatoes, cored and quartered

2 red onions, sliced into sixths

a good pinch of saffron threads

a few sprigs of fresh thyme

4–5 tablespoons olive oil

120 g/generous 1 cup stoned/ pitted black olives, halved

a small handful of fresh basil leaves, shredded

4 boneless, skinless salmon fillets (about 150 g/5½ oz. each)

sea salt and freshly ground black pepper

For the rouille

200 ml/¾ cup mayonnaise

2–4 garlic cloves, crushed

½ teaspoon paprika

a pinch of cayenne pepper

Serves 4

Preheat the oven to 220°C (425°F) Gas 7.

Combine all of the vegetables in a large roasting tray/ sheet pan. Add the saffron and thyme and a good dose of the olive oil. Toss with your hands to coat evenly. Spread the vegetables out in an even layer and sprinkle with salt.

Bake in the preheated oven for 25–30 minutes, until just browned.

Meanwhile, prepare the rouille. Combine all the ingredients in a small bowl, adding the garlic and cayenne to taste. Mix well, adjust the seasoning if necessary and set aside.

Remove the vegetables from the oven and sprinkle over the olives and basil. Arrange the salmon on top, drizzle a little of the olive oil over each fillet and season with salt and pepper. Return to the oven and bake for about 15 minutes more, until the salmon is just cooked through. Serve immediately, with the rouille on the side for spooning.

salmon, broccoli and potato gratin with pesto

This can be prepared the night or morning before serving. Simply assemble the gratin up to the point of pouring on the cream, cover and refrigerate. I never use green basil pesto from a jar as it cannot compare to real pesto. If you can't get fresh pesto then it's better to replace it in this recipe with some chopped fresh parsley, lots of freshly ground black pepper and 1 tablespoon of grated lemon zest. A different taste, equally nice and an honest one.

975 g/34 oz. waxy potatoes, peeled

a large head of broccoli (about 480 g/17 oz.), separated into florets

400 g/14 oz. boneless, skinless salmon fillet

1 tablespoon olive oil

20 g/¾ oz. fresh breadcrumbs (see note on page 26)

4 tablespoons freshly grated Parmesan

250 ml/1 cup single/light cream

2 tablespoons fresh pesto (see introduction)

4 tablespoons milk

2–3 tablespoons butter, cut into small pieces

sea salt and freshly ground black pepper

a 30 x 20-cm/11¾ x 8-inch baking dish, well buttered

Serves 4–6

Preheat the oven to 200°C (400°F) Gas 6.

Put the potatoes in a large saucepan/pot and add sufficient cold water to cover. Parboil until almost tender when pierced with a knife. Drain. When cool enough to handle slice into ¼-cm/⅛-inch thick rounds.

Bring another saucepan of water to the boil. Add the broccoli and a pinch of salt and cook for 3–4 minutes, until just tender. Drain and let cool. Cut into bite-sized pieces and set aside.

Rub the salmon fillets with the oil and place on a sheet of foil, turned up at the sides to catch any juices, and put it on a baking sheet. Sprinkle with a little salt. Bake in the preheated oven for about 10–15 minutes, until cooked through. Let cool, then flake, removing any small bones and set aside.

In a small bowl, mix together the breadcrumbs and 2 tablespoons of the Parmesan. Season well and set aside. In another bowl, stir together the cream and pesto. Season well and set aside.

To assemble, arrange the potato slices on the bottom of the prepared baking dish in an even layer, sprinkle with salt, the remaining Parmesan and drizzle with the milk. Arrange the broccoli in an even layer on top of the potatoes and season lightly. Top with the cooked salmon in an even layer.

Pour over the pesto and cream mixture. Sprinkle the breadcrumb mixture over the top and dot with butter. Bake in the preheated oven for 25–30 minutes, until just browned and crisp on top. Serve immediately.

tuna noodle casserole

In my childhood, this would have been made with cream of mushroom soup from a can. And the crispy topping could have included crushed potato crisps, depending on the whim of the cook. Given that list of ingredients, it's hard to imagine that anyone has fond nostalgia for this dish, but it is one of those nursery favourites among Americans of a certain generation. Here, it is brought up to date with a freshly-made white sauce, mushrooms and even capers, if you like. Serve with a generous and colourful mixed salad.

Preheat the oven to 180°C (350°F) Gas 4.

Heat the oil in a large frying pan/skillet and add the spring onions/scallions, celery and mushrooms. Cook over medium heat for 3–5 minutes, until soft. Season lightly with salt, stir in the capers (if using) and set aside. Season the breadcrumbs and add the paprika. Set aside.

Cook the pasta according to the package instructions. Drain, toss in a little olive oil and set aside.

Melt the butter in a small saucepan set over low heat. Add the flour and cook, stirring, for 1 minute. Gradually pour in the hot milk, whisking/beating constantly, and simmer until the mixture thickens. Stir in the mustard. Let cool slightly. Taste and adjust the seasoning if necessary.

Put the cooked pasta in the prepared baking dish. Pour over the sauce, mushroom mixture, tuna and parsley and toss to mix well. Spread evenly and sprinkle the seasoned breadcrumbs over the top. Bake in the preheated oven for 20–30 minutes, until browned. Serve immediately with a mixed salad.

2 tablespoons olive oil

3 spring onions/scallions, thinly sliced

1 celery stick/stalk, finely chopped

100 g/1½ cups button mushrooms, thinly sliced

2 tablespoons capers (optional)

150 g/2½ cups fresh breadcrumbs (see note on page 26)

a good pinch of paprika

350 g/12 oz. dried egg tagliatelle

50 g/3½ tablespoons butter

35 g/¼ cup plain/all-purpose flour

600 ml/2½ cups hot milk

1 teaspoon mustard powder

350-g/12-oz. can tuna in oil, drained and flaked

a large handful of fresh flat-leaf parsley leaves, chopped

sea salt and freshly ground black pepper

a 30 x 20-cm/11¾ x 8-inch baking dish, well buttered

Serves 4

smoked trout hash with horseradish cream

A perfect dish for two which is speedy to make and satisfying to eat. It could almost be accused of being too simple but the horseradish cream dresses it up nicely. This really is a meal in itself, but you could serve with crusty bread and a peppery watercress salad.

500 g/18 oz. baby new potatoes, scrubbed

2 tablespoons unsalted butter

2–3 tablespoons olive oil

1 small red onion, finely chopped

1 celery stick/stalk, finely chopped

½ teaspoon paprika

1 tablespoon chopped fresh dill

1 tablespoon grated lemon zest

250 g/9 oz. smoked trout, cut in bite-sized pieces

sea salt and freshly ground black pepper

lemon wedges, to serve

Horseradish cream

4–5 tablespoons sour cream or Greek yoghurt

2 teaspoons creamed horseradish

a small bunch of fresh chives, snipped

Serves 2

Put the potatoes in a large saucepan/pot with sufficient water to cover. Add a pinch of salt and boil until tender when pierced with a knife. Drain. When cool enough to handle, cut into cubes.

Meanwhile, make the horseradish cream. Combine the sour cream, horseradish and chives in a small bowl. Mix, cover and set aside.

Melt the butter and 1 tablespoon of the oil in a large frying pan/skillet. Add the cubed potatoes with a pinch of salt and cook, stirring occasionally, for about 10 minutes, until browned.

Add the onion, celery, paprika, dill and lemon zest to the pan and cook, stirring occasionally, for 5 minutes more. Stir in the trout, season, and add a little more oil if the mixture seems dry. Continue cooking, turning every so often, until the hash is well browned.

Serve immediately with the horseradish cream for spooning and lemon wedges.

Vegetarian option: Replace the trout with diced green (bell) pepper and/or cooked broad/fava beans. Serve either variation with a fried egg on top and a dash of Tabasco can replace the horseradish.

smoked salmon spaghetti bake with lemon and dill

This is a fantastic dish when you want something elegant but most of all, quick. It is an economical way to serve smoked salmon too as it calls for trimmings, which are just as flavourful as whole slices. This recipe also works with flaked hot smoked salmon if you prefer a richer flavour.

Preheat the oven to 200°C (400°F) Gas 6.

Cook the spaghetti according to the packet/package instructions. Drain, toss in a little oil and set aside.

In a large bowl, combine the crème fraîche or sour cream, milk and egg and whisk/beat to blend. Stir in the salmon, dill, lemon zest, ½ teaspoon salt and peas and mix to blend. Add the cooked spaghetti, toss well to coat and transfer to the prepared baking dish.

In a small bowl, combine the breadcrumbs and Parmesan and season well. Mix then sprinkle over the spaghetti.

Bake in the preheated oven for 25–35 minutes, until just golden. Serve immediately.

400 g/14 oz. dried spaghetti

400-g/1-lb. tub half-fat crème fraîche or sour cream

165 ml/scant ¾ cup milk

1 egg, beaten

250 g/1½ cups smoked salmon/lox trimmings

a large handful of fresh dill, chopped

1 tablespoon grated lemon zest

75 g/½ cup frozen peas

100 g/1¾ cups fresh breadcrumbs (see note on page 26)

2 tablespoons freshly grated Parmesan

sea salt and freshly ground black pepper

a 30 x 20-cm/11¾ x 8-inch baking dish, well buttered

Serves 4

baked prawns and orzo
with tomatoes, herbs and feta

The combination of seafood and feta has always intrigued me, and this is a recipe
I vaguely knew about, but never actually researched until writing this book. It has been
adjusted, to be served all in one dish, but try it and you will see it has made the transition
very well. Since this is Greek in inspiration, serve with warmed pitta bread and a mixed
salad made with crisp cos lettuce, cucumbers, green (bell) peppers, tomatoes and black
olives. If you prepare the orzo and the tomato sauce ahead, this becomes an unusual
and quick weeknight supper, requiring very little effort to assemble and put on the table.

300 g/2½ cups orzo
(see note on page 50)

2 tablespoons olive oil

1 onion, chopped

2 garlic cloves, crushed

1 teaspoon dried oregano

400-g/14-oz. can chopped
tomatoes

a pinch of sugar

a pinch of allspice

125 ml/½ cup dry white wine

200 ml/scant 1 cup Greek yoghurt

200 g/3½ oz. feta

a small handful of fresh dill,
finely chopped

a small handful of fresh basil
leaves, shredded

500 g/18 oz. raw large prawns/
jumbo shrimp, peeled

a small handful of fresh
mint leaves

sea salt and freshly ground
black pepper

*a 25-cm/9¾-inch round
baking dish*

Serves 4–6

Cook the orzo in a large saucepan/pot of boiling salted
water until tender, 12–15 minutes. Drain and set aside.

Put the oil in a large frying pan/skillet and add the onion.
Cook for 3–5 minutes, until soft. Add the garlic, a pinch
of salt and ½ teaspoon of the oregano and cook, stirring
for 1 minute. Add the tomatoes, sugar, allspice and
wine. Bring to the boil, then reduce the heat and simmer
gently, uncovered, for 10 minutes. Taste and adjust the
seasoning if necessary.

Preheat the oven to 200°C (400°F) Gas 6.

In a small bowl, stir together the yoghurt, half of the feta
(crumbled well) and the remaining oregano. Set aside.

Stir in the dill, basil, prawns/shrimp and the remaining
feta. Add a good pinch of salt. Transfer to the dish and
spread well.

Transfer spoonfuls of the yoghurt mixture, and spread on
top of the prawns/shrimp. This is slightly messy, but it
is okay to leave a few gaps around the edges and in other
places. Sprinkle with the mint leaves and top with a
generous grinding of black pepper. Bake in the preheated
oven for about 30 minutes, until bubbling around the
edges. Serve immediately with a crisp mixed salad.

Moroccan prawn ragout

It's hard to find a recipe that is quicker to make than this one; it is aromatic, out of the ordinary and can be on the table in under thirty minutes. Serve with couscous or rice and a crisp green salad.

4 tablespoons olive oil

1–2 shallots, halved and sliced

2 teaspoons ground cumin

1 teaspoon ground ginger

a pinch of ground saffron

1 teaspoon paprika

1 teaspoon harissa paste

2 garlic cloves, finely chopped

400-g/14-oz. can chopped tomatoes

700 g/25 oz. raw large prawns/ jumbo shrimp, peeled

freshly squeezed juice of ½ a lemon

a large handful of fresh coriander/cilantro leaves, chopped

a large handful of fresh flat-leaf parsley leaves, chopped

sea salt and freshly ground black pepper

couscous or rice, to serve

lemon wedges, to serve

Serves 4

Heat the oil in a large frying pan/skillet. Add the shallots and cook over low heat for 2–3 minutes, until softened. Add the cumin, ginger, saffron, paprika, harissa and garlic and cook, stirring for 1 minute. Do not let the garlic burn.

Add the tomatoes and 125 ml/½ cup water and season well. Simmer gently, uncovered, for at least 15 minutes. Taste and adjust the seasoning if necessary. (The recipe can be made in advance up to this point.)

Stir in the prawns/shrimp and cook, uncovered, for about 5 minutes, until opaque. Remove from the heat, squeeze over the lemon juice and add the parsley and coriander/ cilantro. Mix well and serve immediately spooned over couscous or rice, as preferred, with lemon wedges on the side, to squeeze over.

Spanish seafood stew

Here's a one-pot dinner that will fill your kitchen with enticing smells from faraway places. You will need a deep saucepan to accommodate all the ingredients, including the mussels at the end. If you do not have one, the mussels can be steamed on their own; simply add them and their cooking liquor into the main dish before serving. The only other requirement is a basket of crusty bread to help mop up the sauce and garlicky mayonnaise.

1 teaspoon cumin seeds

2 tablespoons olive oil

1 large onion, halved and sliced

2 red (bell) peppers, halved, deseeded and sliced

4 ripe tomatoes, peeled, deseeded and chopped

2 anchovy fillets, finely chopped

1–2 fresh green chillies/chiles, sliced

3 garlic cloves, sliced

1.5 kg/3½ lb. new potatoes, peeled and cut into wedges

250 ml/1 cup dry white wine

350 ml/1½ cups fish stock

1 bay leaf

500 g/18 oz. live mussels

400 g/14 oz. firm-fleshed white fish, such as cod or haddock

250 g/9 oz. raw large prawns/ jumbo shrimp, peeled

a large handful of fresh flat-leaf parsley leaves, chopped

sea salt and freshly ground black pepper

alioli or rouille (see page 93), to serve

Serves 4

Put the cumin seeds in a small non-stick frying pan/ skillet and dry roast over medium heat until they just turn brown and become aromatic. Crush to a fine powder using a mortar and pestle. Set aside.

Heat the oil in a large, deep saucepan with a lid. Add the onion and (bell) peppers and cook for 3–5 minutes, until soft. Add the tomatoes, anchovies, chillies/chiles, garlic, cumin and potatoes. Season with salt and stir to combine.

Add the wine, stock and bay leaf. Bring to the boil and cook for 1 minute, then lower the heat and simmer gently, uncovered, for 20–30 minutes, until the potatoes are tender when pierced with a knife. Taste for seasoning and adjust if necessary. (Up to this point, the recipe can be made one day in advance.)

Clean and debeard the mussels and discard any that do not close. Stir in the fish and prawns/shrimp and cook until just opaque. Increase the heat to high. Add the mussels on top, cover and cook for 2–3 minutes, until the mussels open. (Discard any that do not open.)

Sprinkle with the parsley and serve, with the alioli or the rouille for spooning and plenty of crusty bread.

seafood lasagna

2 tablespoons olive oil

1 onion, chopped

1 celery stick/stalk, diced

2 garlic cloves, finely chopped

½ teaspoon dried chilli/
hot red pepper flakes

a sprig of fresh thyme

a large handful of fresh flat-leaf
parsley leaves, chopped

400 g/14 oz. mixed seafood
(prawns/shrimp, scallops and
squid rings)

125 ml/½ cup dry white wine

700-g/1½-lb. bottle passata
(Italian strained tomatoes)

a pinch of sugar

8 sheets green lasagne

3 tablespoons freshly grated
Parmesan

sea salt and freshly ground
black pepper

For the béchamel

50 g/3½ tablespoons butter

5 tablespoons plain/all-purpose
flour

600 ml/2½ cups hot milk

2 tablespoons grated Parmesan

3 tablespoons mascarpone

a pinch of ground nutmeg

200 g/1 cup frozen leaf spinach,
defrosted

*a 30 x 20-cm/11¾ x 8-inch
baking dish*

Serves 4–6

A more summery version of a family favourite, this lasagne has shellfish, spinach and a béchamel made even richer with mascarpone. Serve with a salad dressed with vinaigrette.

Preheat the oven to 190°C (375°F) Gas 5.

Heat the oil in a large frying pan/skillet. Add the onion and celery and cook over low heat for 3–5 minutes, until soft. Stir in the garlic, dried chilli/hot red pepper flakes, thyme and parsley and season generously with salt. Cook, stirring, for 1 minute. Add the seafood and cook, stirring, for 1 minute. Add the wine and cook for 1 minute more. Add the passata, season with salt and add the sugar. Stir to blend and simmer gently, uncovered, for 15 minutes.

To make the béchamel, melt the butter in a heavy-based saucepan set over low heat. Stir in the flour and cook, stirring constantly, for 1 minute. Add the hot milk gradually, whisking/beating constantly. Continue whisking/beating for 3–5 minutes, until the sauce begins to thicken. Season and stir in the Parmesan and mascarpone until blended. Stir in the nutmeg and spinach.

To assemble, spoon a thin layer of the seafood sauce on the bottom of the baking dish. Return any bits of seafood to the sauce; you just want a thin layer of tomato base for the pasta to sit on. Top with 2 sheets of lasagne. Spread half of the seafood sauce on top, spreading evenly right up to the edges and distribute the seafood evenly on top. Top with 2 sheets of lasagne. Spread half of the béchamel sauce on top, spreading evenly right up to the edges. Continue layering (lasagne, seafood, lasagne, béchamel) and finish with the béchamel.

Sprinkle with the Parmesan. Bake in the preheated oven for 25–25 minutes, until just browned. Serve immediately.

vegetarian

baked rigatoni
with mozzarella

Blissfully simple to make, with virtuous quantities of vegetables, this is a good way to eat well with minimal effort. And putting the mozzarella in the middle as well as on top means you get a lovely inner layer of melting cheese, as well as a browned topping. Other vegetables can be used according to what's in season or to hand – courgettes/zucchini, sweetcorn, broccoli, spinach and will all work nicely. The important thing is to chop the vegetables to the same size, to allow them to nestle inside the pasta shapes.

3 tablespoons olive oil

1 small onion, diced

1 carrot, finely diced

2–3 celery sticks/stalks, from the inner section, with leaves, diced

1 small red, yellow or orange (bell) pepper, deseeded and diced

100 g/1½ cups diced mushrooms

3 garlic cloves, finely chopped

125 ml/½ cup dry white or red wine

½–1 teaspoon dried chilli/hot red pepper flakes, to taste

½ tablespoon fresh thyme leaves or 1 teaspoon dried thyme

a large handful of fresh flat-leaf parsley or basil leaves, finely chopped

400-g/14-oz. can chopped tomatoes

700-g/1½-lb. bottle passata (Italian strained tomatoes)

a pinch of sugar

500 g/6 cups dried rigatoni

500 g/18 oz. mozzarella, sliced

sea salt and freshly ground black pepper

a 30 x 20-cm/11¾ x 8-inch baking dish, well oiled

Serves 4–6

Heat the oil in a large saucepan/pot, add the onion and cook over low heat for 3–5 minutes, until soft. Add the carrot, celery and (bell) pepper. Season and cook for 2–3 minutes. Stir in the mushrooms and garlic and cook for 1 minute more. Add the wine and cook for 1 minute more. Stir in the dried chilli/hot red pepper flakes, thyme, parsley, tomatoes, passata and sugar. Season generously and stir to mix. Reduce the heat and simmer, uncovered, for about 20–30 minutes. Taste and adjust the seasoning if necessary.

Meanwhile, cook the pasta according to the package instructions until al dente. Drain well and set aside.

Preheat the oven to 200°C (400°F) Gas 6.

Combine the cooked pasta and the vegetable sauce and mix well. Spread half the pasta in the prepared dish evenly. Top with half of the mozzarella. Top with the remaining pasta in an even layer and arrange the remaining mozzarella slices on top.

Bake in the preheated oven for 25–30 minutes, until the cheese melts and bubbles. Serve immediately.

vegetable enchiladas

2 tablespoons olive oil

450 g/1 lb. courgettes/zucchini, diced

1 red onion, diced

150 g/1 cup sweetcorn kernels

½ fresh red or green chilli/chile, halved, deseeded and sliced

1 teaspoon ground cumin

400-g/14-oz. can black beans, drained

a handful of fresh coriander/cilantro leaves, chopped

8 corn tortillas

250 g/9 oz. mild Cheddar, grated

sour cream, to serve

For the sauce

1 onion, coarsely chopped

2 garlic cloves

2 tablespoons olive oil

1–2 teaspoons dried chilli/hot red pepper flakes, to taste

½ teaspoon Spanish hot smoked paprika (pimentón picante)

1 teaspoon ground cumin

1 teaspoon dried oregano

700-g/1½-lb. bottle passata (Italian strained tomatoes)

1 vegetable stock cube diluted in 375 ml/1½ cups hot water

sea salt and freshly ground black pepper

a 35 x 25-cm/14 x 11¾-inch baking dish

Serves 4

Home-made enchiladas are so much easier to make than you think and very delicious.

Preheat the oven to 200°C (400°F) Gas 6.

To make the sauce, put the onion and garlic in a food processor and pulse until finely chopped. Transfer to a large frying pan/skillet. Add the oil and cook over low heat, stirring, for 3–5 minutes, until just soft. Stir in the dried chilli/hot red pepper flakes, paprika, cumin and oregano and add salt to taste. Cook, stirring, for 2 minutes. Add the passata and stock and simmer gently, uncovered, for at least 15 minutes. Let cool slightly.

Meanwhile, make the filling. Heat the oil in a large saucepan/pot, add the courgettes/zucchini and onion and cook over low heat for 5–8 minutes, until just tender. Stir in the sweetcorn, chilli/chile, cumin and beans and season to taste. Remove from the heat and stir in the coriander/cilantro, reserving some to garnish.

To assemble, warm the tortillas according to the package instructions. Coat the bottom of a baking dish with a layer of the tomato sauce. Working one at a time, dab a tortilla gently in the warm sauce in the pan, just to coat the bottom side, then turn over to coat the other side. (If you use tongs for this, be careful not to tear the tortillas.)

Transfer the coated tortilla to a plate and fill with a large spoonful of filling, a handful of grated cheese, then fold the tortilla over to enclose the filling and transfer it in a baking dish, seam-side down. Continue until all the tortillas have been filled. Spoon the remaining sauce over the tortillas, concentrating on the ends as these tend to dry out. Sprinkle the remaining cheese down the centre.

Bake in the preheated oven for 15–20 minutes, until the cheese has melted. Sprinkle with the reserved coriander/cilantro and serve with sour cream on the side.

courgette gratin with fresh herbs and goats' cheese

A classic of French home cooking, this gratin includes a topping of tangy goats' cheese. If you grow your own herbs, add whatever is on offer: savory, majoram, oregano or any other soft-leaved herb, the more the merrier. This is perfect, simply served with a mixed salad of lettuce and ripe tomatoes and a big basket of fresh crusty bread.

250 ml/1 cup double/ heavy cream

leaves from a small bunch of fresh flat-leaf parsley, finely chopped

a small bunch of chives, snipped

a pinch of freshly grated nutmeg

75 g/2½ oz. Gruyère, grated

1.5 kg/3¼ lb. courgettes/ zucchini, very thinly sliced

150 g/5½ oz. soft goats' cheese

sea salt and freshly ground black pepper

a 24-cm/9½-inch round, deep-sided baking dish, well buttered

Serves 4

Preheat the oven to 190°C (375°F) Gas 5.

Put the cream, parsley, chives, nutmeg, salt and pepper in a small bowl and whisk/beat together. Add half the Gruyère.

Arrange half the courgette/zucchini slices in the prepared baking dish, sprinkle with the remaining Gruyère and season with a little salt. Top with the remaining courgette/zucchini slices, season again and pour over the cream mixture. Crumble the goats' cheese over the top.

Bake in the preheated oven for 35–45 minutes, until browned. Serve immediately with a mixed salad and plenty of crusty bread.

Note: If preferred, you can make the gratin in 4 individual dishes, simply reduce the cooking time by about 5–10 minutes.

root vegetable gratin

There is something very satisfying and tranquil about preparing this recipe. So if the thought of peeling and slicing these vegetables puts you off, think again. It sounds perhaps more daunting than it really is; but you will be done in no time, and it will be well worth the effort. This is a very simple dish, very impressive and hugely delightful. Serve with a cheese platter, crusty bread and a green salad.

Preheat the oven to 200°C (400°F) Gas 6.

Put all the prepared vegetable slices in a large bowl and toss gently to combine. Set aside.

Combine the cream, crème fraîche or sour cream and milk in a small saucepan and heat just to melt the crème fraîche or sour cream. Stir well and season with salt and pepper.

Arrange half of the vegetables slices in the prepared baking dish. Sprinkle with a little salt and one-third of the cheese. Pour over one-third of the cream mixture. Top with the rest of the vegetable slices, the remaining cheese and a sprinkle of salt. Pour over the remaining cream mixture and bake in the preheated oven for 1–1½ hours, until browned on top. Serve immediately.

3 small turnips
(about 375 g/13 oz.), peeled,
halved and very thinly sliced

½ a celeriac/celery root
(about 325 g/11½ oz.), peeled,
halved and very thinly sliced

½ a swede/rutabaga
(about 450 g/1 lb.), peeled,
halved and very thinly sliced

650 g/23 oz. waxy potatoes,
peeled, halved and very thinly
sliced

225 ml/scant 1 cup double/
heavy cream

100 g/½ cup crème fraîche
or sour cream

250 ml/1 cup milk

125 g/4½ oz. Gruyère or
medium Cheddar, grated

sea salt and freshly ground
black pepper

*a 30 x 20-cm/11¾ x 8-inch
baking dish, very well buttered*

Serves 4–6

ravioli bake with grilled sweet peppers

An easy dinner dish made with my favourite freezer staple: mixed grilled/broiled (bell) peppers. These are fantastic for stirring into anything that needs a quick lift but if you cannot find any, thinly slice a red and a yellow (bell) pepper and sweat it with the onions. This is meant to be simple, so the ingredient list is kept short, but some sliced mushrooms and stoned/pitted black olives make a pleasant addition if you have some. Fresh or dried ravioli both work well, and any filling will do, but goats' cheese and pesto is an especially good one. Serve with a simple green salad.

2 tablespoons olive oil

1 onion, halved and sliced

225 g/½ lb. frozen mixed grilled (bell) peppers (see recipe introduction)

3 garlic cloves, crushed

1 teaspoon dried thyme

¼–½ teaspoon dried chilli/ hot red pepper flakes, to taste

2 x 400-g/14-oz. cans chopped tomatoes

a pinch of sugar

a large handful of fresh basil or flat-leaf parsley leaves, chopped

500 g/18 oz. small filled ravioli or cappeletti

75 g/2½ oz. Gruyère or medium Cheddar, grated

2 tablespoons freshly grated Parmesan

sea salt and freshly ground black pepper

a 33 x 21-cm/13 x 8¼-inch baking dish, lightly oiled

Serves 4–6

Preheat the oven to 200°C (400°F) Gas 6.

Heat the oil in a large saucepan/pot. Add the onion and cook over low heat for 3–5 minutes, until soft. Add the (bell) peppers, garlic, thyme and chilli/hot red pepper flakes and cook, stirring, for 2–3 minutes. Stir in the tomatoes and sugar, and season and simmer, uncovered, for about 15 minutes. Taste and adjust the seasoning if necessary. Stir in the basil.

Cook the ravioli according to the package instructions and drain well.

Tip the cooked ravioli into the sauce and stir gently to coat. Transfer to the prepared baking dish, spread evenly and sprinkle both the cheeses over the top.

Bake in the preheated oven for 20–30 minutes, until the cheese is melted and golden. Serve immediately with a green salad.

artichoke, mushroom and olive pasta bake with provolone

Here is a great vegetarian dish, with so much flavour no one will miss the meat! This recipe calls for provolone which is a smoked Italian cheese, but almost any cheese can be used so experiment with different types – Gruyère is a great one here, as is smoked mozzarella, soft goats' cheese or even mature Cheddar. Serve with a crisp green salad.

2–3 tablespoons olive oil

1 onion, finely chopped

½ teaspoon each dried oregano and dried thyme

130 g/2 cups coarsley chopped white mushrooms

4 garlic cloves, crushed

¼ teaspoon dried chilli/hot red pepper flakes

125 ml/½ cup dry white

2 x 400-g/14-oz. cans chopped tomatoes

400-g/14-oz. can artichoke hearts, drained and sliced

50 g/½ cup stoned/pitted black olives, sliced

a pinch of sugar

400 g/4 cups dried penne

150 g/5½ oz. provolone, cubed

Béchamel sauce

50 g/3½ tablespoons butter

35 g/¼ cup plain/all-purpose flour

600 ml/2½ cups hot milk

4 tablespoons grated Parmesan

sea salt and freshly ground black pepper

a 30 x 20-cm/11¾ x 8-inch baking dish

Serves 4

Heat 1 tablespoon of the oil in a large frying pan/ skillet. Add the onion and cook over low heat for about 5 minutes, until soft. Stir in the oregano, thyme and mushrooms and cook for 2–3 minutes more, adding a little more oil if required. Stir in the garlic and dried chilli/hot red pepper flakes and season with salt. Cook for 1 minute, then add the wine. Cook for 1 minute more, then add the tomatoes, artichokes and olives. Add the sugar, season, stir to combine and simmer for about 15 minutes. Taste and adjust the seasoning if necessary.

Preheat the oven to 200°C (400°F) Gas 6.

To prepare the béchamel sauce, melt the butter in a heavy-based saucepan set over low heat. Add the flour and cook, stirring, for 1 minute. Slowly pour in the hot milk, whisking/beating continuously, and simmer until the mixture thickens. Season well. Stir in 2 tablespoons of the Parmesan and set aside.

Cook the pasta according the package instructions until just al dente. Drain. To assemble, spread a small amount of the tomato mixture over the bottom of the baking dish and add 1 tablespoon of the oil. Arrange about one-third of the cooked pasta in a single layer on the bottom. Top with half of the remaining tomato mixture and spread evenly. Cover with another layer of pasta (using half of the remaining amount). Spoon over half of the béchamel and spread evenly. Top with the provolone, spacing the pieces evenly. Spoon the remaining tomato mixture on top. Top with the remaining pasta and béchamel. Sprinkle with the remaining Parmesan. Bake in the preheated oven for about 30–40 minutes, until browned. Serve immediately.

butternut squash, sweetcorn and bread pudding with cheese and chives

Inspiration for this recipe comes from an old, well-worn vegetarian cookbook of mine. It is a recipe for savoury bread pudding/bake, but adding a few vegetables makes it more of a meal, and the sweetness of the squash and sweetcorn go well with the creamy, cheesy bread part. In place of the baguette, you could save up the ends from sliced loaves. And any kind of cheese can be used here, as can a combination of cheeses, so it's a good way to use up odds and ends. Serve with a mixed salad.

1 tablespoon olive oil

1 large onion, halved and thinly sliced

375 ml/generous 1½ cups milk

225 ml/scant 1 cup single/light cream

3 eggs, beaten

a small bunch of chives, snipped

leaves from a small bunch of fresh flat-leaf parsley, finely chopped

1 baguette, cut into ½-cm/¼-inch slices

300 g/2 cups sweetcorn kernels

about 500 g/18 oz. peeled and sliced butternut squash

100 g/3½ oz. mature/sharp Cheddar, grated

sea salt and freshly ground black pepper

a 30 x 20-cm/11¾ x 8-inch baking dish, very well buttered

Serves 4–6

Preheat the oven to 190°C (375°F) Gas 5.

Heat the oil in a large frying pan/skillet. Add the onion and cook over low heat for 3–5 minutes, until soft. Season lightly and set aside.

Combine the milk, cream and eggs in a small bowl and whisk/beat to combine. Season with 1½ teaspoons salt. Add the chives and parsley, mix well and set aside.

Arrange half the baguette slices in the prepared baking dish in a single layer; you may need to tear some to cover all the space. Put half of the onion slices on top, then scatter over half of the sweetcorn. Arrange half of the squash slices evenly on top and sprinkle with half of the cheese. Repeat one more time (bread, onion, sweetcorn, squash, cheese). Stir the milk mixture and pour it evenly all over the pudding.

Cover tightly with foil and bake in the preheated oven for 20 minutes. Remove the foil and continue baking for about 30–40 minutes, until golden. Serve immediately.

Provençal aubergine, tomato and onion bake

This indulgent French vegetable dish improves with time so perfect for making ahead, or cooking extra for leftovers. A bowl of pasta tossed with cream and finely grated Parmesan is the perfect accompaniment.

about 125 ml/½ cup olive oil

4 garlic cloves, crushed

400-g/14-oz. can chopped tomatoes

a pinch of sugar

1 tablespoon chopped fresh flat-leaf parsley leaves

a pinch of cayenne pepper

4 medium aubergines/eggplant, sliced

75 g/1½ cups fresh breadcrumbs (see note on page 26)

leaves stripped from 2 sprigs of fresh thyme or 1 teaspoon dried thyme

2 large onions, thickly sliced

3 large or 5 medium fresh plum tomatoes, sliced

leaves from 2 sprigs of fresh basil, finely chopped

sea salt and freshly ground black pepper

a 30 x 20-cm/11¾ x 8-inch baking dish

Serves 4–6

Heat 1 tablespoon of the oil in a saucepan. Add the garlic and cook over medium heat for 1 minute; taking care not to let it burn. Add the tomatoes, sugar, parsley and cayenne and season well. Simmer, uncovered, for at least 15 minutes.

Preheat the oven to 200°C (400°F) Gas 6.

Bring a large saucepan/pot of salted water to the boil and add the aubergine/eggplant. Cook for 3–5 minutes, to blanch. Remove and pat dry on kitchen paper/paper towels.

Combine the breadcrumbs and thyme leaves in a small bowl and season. Toss to mix and set aside.

Drizzle 2–3 tablespoons of oil in the baking dish and spread evenly. Arrange the aubergine/eggplant slices on top and drizzle with some more oil. Arrange the onion slices on top and season. Spoon the tomato mixture on top of the onions and spread evenly. Arrange the tomato slices on top and then sprinkle with the breadcrumb mixture.

Bake in the preheated oven for about 45 minutes, until browned. Serve hot or warm.

couscous with seven vegetables

This is a vegetarian version of a traditional Moroccan dish, which is meant to be highly aromatic and slightly sweet. It can be made with other vegetables: pumpkin, squash and turnip are all suitable additions, but seven vegetables is considered good luck so if you experiment with others be sure to maintain the numbers. It is a meal in itself but you could also serve it to accompany simply grilled/broiled chicken or lamb.

3 courgettes/zucchini, halved and quartered lengthways

3 large fresh plum tomatoes, halved and deseeded

1 red (bell) pepper, cored, deseeded and quartered

1 yellow (bell) pepper, cored, deseeded and quartered

1–2 tablespoons olive oil

1 litre/4 cups vegetable stock

a pinch of saffron threads

½ teaspoon ground turmeric

1 teaspoon ground white pepper

½ teaspoon cinnamon

1 teaspoon ground ginger

a small bunch of fresh coriander/cilantro, tied firmly in a bundle with string

3 large onions, quartered

4 large carrots, peeled, halved and quartered

500 g/18 oz. swede/rutabaga, peeled and cubed

200-g/7-oz. can chickpeas, drained

a large handful of raisins

1–2 teaspoons harissa paste, to taste

freshly squeezed lemon juice

250 g/1½ cups couscous

sea salt

Serves 4

Preheat the oven to 220°C (425°F) Gas 7.

Arrange the courgettes/zucchini, tomatoes and (bell) peppers in a large roasting pan. Drizzle with the oil and toss to coat. Spread out in a single layer, sprinkle lightly with salt and roast in the preheated oven for 20–30 minutes, until browned. Remove from the oven, transfer the vegetables to a large plate, cover with foil to keep warm and set aside.

Meanwhile combine the stock, saffron, turmeric, pepper, cinnamon, ginger, coriander/cilantro bundle, onions, carrots and swede/rutabaga in a large saucepan/pot. Top up with a bit more water if necessary; the vegetables should be covered but not completely submerged. Season with salt and bring to the boil, then reduce the heat and simmer gently, uncovered, for about 30 minutes. Stir in the chickpeas and raisins and continue simmering for 10–15 minutes, until the vegetables are tender and the liquid has reduced by about one-third.

Meanwhile prepare the couscous according to the packet instructions. Cover with foil and keep warm in a low oven until ready to serve.

Use a slotted spoon to transfer the stewed vegetables to the plate with the roasted vegetables and toss gently to combine. Add the harissa paste and a squeeze of lemon juice to the broth in the saucepan and stir to blend. Taste and adjust the seasoning if necessary. Pour the broth over the vegetables and serve them spooned over the couscous.

roasted butternut squash with spiced lentils, goats' cheese and walnuts

This recipe will fill your kitchen with appetizing and exotic aromas. You can use pumpkin or sweet potato in place of the squash, or a combination of the two, as long as the weight is roughly the same as that of a butternut squash. Sometimes I add a handful of canned chickpeas during the last bit of simmering. Serve with plenty of crusty bread.

275 g/1½ cups dried green lentils, rinsed and drained

50 g/½ cup walnut pieces

1 butternut squash, peeled, deseeded and cubed

3 tablespoons olive oil

1 large onion, halved and sliced

1 fresh red chilli/chile, halved, deseeded and sliced

1 teaspoon ground cumin

1 teaspoon ground turmeric

1 teaspoon paprika

2 garlic cloves, crushed

400-g/14-oz. can chopped tomatoes

a pinch of sugar

a large handful of fresh flat-leaf parsley leaves, chopped

a small handful of fresh coriander/cilantro leaves, finely chopped

freshly squeezed juice of ½ a lemon

250 g/9 oz. soft goats' cheese or feta

sea salt and freshly ground black pepper

Serves 4

Preheat the oven to 190°C (375°F) Gas 5.

Put the lentils in a saucepan with sufficient cold water to cover. Add a pinch of salt, bring to the boil and simmer for 20–30 minutes, until tender. Drain and set aside.

Dry roast the walnuts in a small non-stick frying pan/skillet set over low heat, until browned. Set aside.

Arrange the squash cubes on a baking sheet, toss with 2 tablespoons of the oil and sprinkle with a little salt. Roast in the preheated oven for 30–35 minutes, until tender, turning halfway through cooking time.

Heat the remaining oil in a large saucepan/pot, add the onion and cook over low heat for 3–5 minutes, until soft. Add the chilli/chile, cumin, turmeric, paprika, garlic and a pinch of salt and cook, stirring for 1 minute. Add the tomatoes, sugar, another pinch of salt, half the parsley and half the coriander/cilantro. Simmer, uncovered, for 20 minutes, stirring in the cooked lentils about 5 minutes before the end of cooking time, just to warm through. Taste and adjust the seasoning if necessary.

Add the roasted squash, the remaining herbs and a squeeze of lemon juice. Taste and adjust the seasoning. Crumble over the goats' cheese, add the walnuts and serve immediately with plenty of crusty bread.

wild mushroom and potato ragout with leek

So many potato recipes are baked or roasted, but it's nice to have a stovetop preparation. This one is a lovely, autumnal/fall dish that is quick to throw together, so perfect for a midweek supper, just the thing when days and nights are getting cooler. Chanterelles are a favourite mushroom of mine, but any kind can be used here, including dried mushrooms, but these will need to be soaked in warm water beforehand.

1 kg/2¼ lb. new potatoes

2 tablespoons olive oil

1 onion, halved and sliced

1 trimmed leek, thinly sliced into rounds

2 tablespoons unsalted butter

300 g/10½ oz. chanterelle mushrooms, cut into bite-sized pieces

2 garlic cloves, crushed

1 teaspoon dried thyme

400 ml/scant 1¾ cups vegetable stock

1 bay leaf

2 tablespoons crème fraîche or sour cream

a large handful of fresh flat-leaf parsley leaves, chopped

sea salt and freshly ground black pepper

Serves 4

Put the potatoes in a large saucepan/pot with sufficient water to cover. Add a pinch of salt and bring to the boil. Cook until tender when pierced with a knife. When cool enough to handle, cut into large dice.

Heat the oil in a large saucepan/pot and add the onion and leek. Season lightly and cook over medium heat for 2–3 minutes, until soft.

Add the butter and stir until melted. Add the mushrooms, garlic and thyme. Cook, stirring, for 1–2 minutes. Season lightly, then add the stock, bay leaf and cooked potatoes. Add a little water to just cover if necessary.

Simmer, uncovered, for 30–40 minutes, until the liquid has reduced by half. Taste and adjust the seasoning if necessary. Stir in the crème fraîche or sour cream and parsley and serve immediately.

cannellini bean and cabbage gratin

This is good, reliable comfort food, ideal for adding a bit of warmth on a chilly evening. This makes a good vegetarian main dish but is also a nice companion for sausages, roast lamb or even duck. Although there are carrots in the recipe, I find this works well with a few more on the side, either roasted or mashed with a little butter.

Bring a large saucepan/pot water to the boil. Add the cabbage and a pinch of salt and cook for 5–8 minutes, until just blanched. Drain and set aside.

Heat the oil in a large frying pan/skillet. Add the onion and cook over low heat for 3–5 minutes, until soft. Add the carrots and celery and cook for 5 minutes more. Season well, add the garlic and cook for 1 minute. Add the beans, thyme, bay leaf, rosemary, sage and wine. Bring to the boil and simmer, uncovered, for about 10 minutes, until the liquid has almost reduced.

In a small bowl, mix the breadcrumbs and Parmesan and season well. Set aside.

Preheat the oven to 200°C (400°F) Gas 6.

Core and chop the blanched cabbage and add to the beans with the stock. Cover and simmer for 10 minutes, then uncover and simmer until the liquid is reduced by half. Stir in the crème fraîche or sour cream. Taste and adjust the seasoning if necessary.

Transfer the mixture to the baking dish and spread evenly. Arrange the tomato slices on top and sprinkle over the seasoned breadcrumbs. Bake in the preheated oven for about 20–25 minutes, until browned. Serve immediately.

½ a savoy cabbage, cut in half

2 tablespoons olive oil

1 onion, chopped

2 carrots, peeled and sliced

2 celery sticks/stalks, sliced

4 garlic cloves, sliced

2 x 400-g/14-oz. cans cannellini beans, drained

½ teaspoon dried thyme

1 bay leaf

leaves from a sprig of fresh rosemary or sage (or both)

125 ml/½ cup dry white wine

100 g/2 cups fresh breadcrumbs (see note on page 26)

2 tablespoons grated Parmesan

300 ml/1¼ cups vegetable stock

2 tablespoons crème fraîche

5 fresh plum tomatoes, sliced

sea salt and freshly ground black pepper

a 24-cm/9½-inch round baking dish

Serves 4–6

Greek summer vegetable stew with lemon and olives

Any kind of olive can be used here but if you can find some marinated with whole coriander seeds, these are the best ones to use. This is a summer stew and is best eaten lukewarm or at room temperature. Serve with a salad made from cos lettuce dressed with extra virgin olive oil and lemon juice, some feta and crusty bread.

2 tablespoons olive oil

1 onion, chopped

500 g/18 oz. small new potatoes (red if available), cubed

350 g/12 oz. courgettes/zucchini, halved and quartered lengthways, then sliced thickly

3 garlic cloves, sliced

¼ teaspoon paprika

¼ teaspoon cayenne pepper

2 x 400-g/14-oz. cans chopped tomatoes

leaves from a small bunch of flat-leaf parsley, finely chopped

sprigs from a small bunch of dill, finely chopped

250 g/1½ cups halved fine green beans

100 g/¾ cup stoned/pitted cracked green olives

freshly squeezed juice of ½ a lemon

sea salt and freshly ground black pepper

Serves 4–6

Heat the oil in a large saucepan/pot. Add the onion and cook over low heat for 3–5 minutes, until soft. Add the potatoes, courgettes/zucchini, garlic, paprika, cayenne and a pinch of salt and cook, stirring to coat in the oil, for 1 minute.

Add the tomatoes, parsley and half the dill. Stir to combine and add some water to thin slightly; about 125 ml/½ cup should be enough. Season well, then cover and simmer for 30 minutes.

Add the green beans, cover and continue to simmer for about 20 minutes more, until the beans are tender. Stir in the olives, lemon juice and remaining dill. Taste and adjust the seasoning if necessary. Serve at room temperature with a simple salad of cos lettuce, some feta cheese and plenty of crusty bread.

sweet potato, spinach and chickpea stew with coconut

This falls somewhere between a stew and a soup, but I like to make use of the abundant sauce and serve with fragrant jasmine rice. If you like things spicy, add two chillies/chiles and all their seeds; if not, add one and keep the seeds out. It will be very mild and the specks of red are pretty against the orange.

1 tablespoon vegetable oil

1 onion, halved and sliced

30-g/1 oz. piece of fresh ginger, peeled and grated

1–2 fresh red chillies/chiles, halved and sliced

1 teaspoon curry powder

1 teaspoon ground cumin

1.3 kg/3 lbs. sweet potatoes, peeled and cubed

400-ml/14-oz. can coconut milk

450 ml/scant 2 cups vegetable stock

1 tablespoon Thai fish sauce (optional)

400-g/14-oz. can chickpeas, drained

225 g/8 oz. fresh baby spinach leaves, washed

sea salt

jasmine rice, to serve

Serves 4–6

Heat the oil in a large saucepan/pot. Add the onion and cook over low heat for 3–5 minutes, until soft. Add the ginger, chillies/chiles, curry powder, cumin and a pinch of salt. Cook for 1–2 minutes, stirring, until aromatic.

Add the sweet potatoes and stir to coat in the spices. Add the coconut milk and stock and a little water if necessary, just to cover the sweet potatoes; the mixture should be soupy as it will cook down. Add the fish sauce (if using) or some salt, if preferred. Bring to the boil, then simmer, uncovered, for 15 minutes.

Add the chickpeas and continue to simmer for about 15–20 minutes more, until the sweet potatoes are tender.

Add the spinach, in batches, stirring to blend and waiting for each batch to wilt before adding the next. Taste and adjust the seasoning if necessary. Serve immediately with jasmine rice.

winter vegetable bake

This is really three recipes in one dish: a potato gratin, cauliflower cheese and roasted Brussels sprouts. The result is substantial and filling, and good served with crusty bread and a salad of robust winter greens. That said, nothing should stop you from serving this alongside a Sunday roast.

280 g/10 oz. Brussels sprouts, trimmed and quartered

2–3 tablespoons olive oil

500 g/18 oz. cauliflower florets (about 1 medium head)

750 g/26 oz. waxy potatoes

200 ml/¾ cup crème fraîche or sour cream

125 ml/½ cup single/ light cream

50 g/1 cup fresh breadcrumbs (see note on page 26)

a pinch of paprika

1 onion, halved and thinly sliced

125 g/4½ oz. mature/sharp Cheddar, grated

2–3 tablespoons grated Parmesan

sea salt and freshly ground black pepper

a 30 x 20-cm/11¾ x 8-inch baking dish, very well buttered

Serves 4–6

Preheat the oven to 200°C (400°F) Gas 6.

Toss the Brussels sprouts with the oil to coat, season with salt and spread in a single layer on a baking sheet. Roast in the preheated oven for 25–30 minutes, until just tender.

Meanwhile, bring a large saucepan/pot of water to the boil. Add the cauliflower florets and a pinch of salt and blanch for 5–8 minutes, until just tender. Drain. When cool enough to handle, slice thinly and set aside.

Bring another large saucepan/pot of salted water to the boil, add the potatoes and cook until just tender when pierced with a knife but not cooked through. Drain. When cool enough to handle, slice the potatoes thinly and set aside.

In a bowl, whisk/beat together the crème fraîche and cream and season well. Set aside. Season the breadcrumbs and stir in the paprika. Set aside.

Arrange the potato slices in the prepared baking dish and lay the onion slices on top. Sprinkle with salt and half of the cheese. Arrange the cauliflower slices on top of the cheese, then sprinkle with the remaining cheese. Pour over the cream mixture. Top with the roasted Brussels sprouts in an even layer, including any leaves that break off. Cover with foil and bake in the preheated oven for 30 minutes. After 30 minutes, remove from the oven. Remove the foil, sprinkle with the breadcrumbs and Parmesan and continue baking, uncovered, for a further 30–40 minutes, until well browned. Serve immediately.

ratatouille

Although this is unashamedly olive oil laden, it shouldn't be greasy, which is difficult as aubergines/eggplant tend to soak up as much oil as they're given. This is why I microwave the aubergines/eggplant to pre-cook them and keep oil absorption to a minimum. Light steaming will have the same effect if you don't have a microwave. Serve with rice and a little grated cheese to make a meal. I always seem to have an awkwardly small amount of ratatouille left, which is happily just enough to fill an omelette or savoury crêpe for two.

1 kg/2¼ lbs. aubergines/eggplant, cut into cubes

6–7 tablespoons olive oil

2 onions, coarsely chopped

2 red (bell) peppers, halved, deseeded and cut into pieces

2 yellow (bell) peppers, halved, deseeded and cut into pieces

1 green (bell) pepper, halved, deseeded and cut into pieces

750 g/26 oz. courgettes/zucchini, halved lengthways and sliced

6 fresh plum tomatoes, halved, deseeded and chopped

6 garlic cloves, crushed

a large handful of fresh basil leaves, coarsely chopped

sea salt and freshly ground black pepper

rice, to serve (optional)

Serves 4–6

Put the aubergine/eggplant cubes in a microwave-proof bowl with 3 tablespoons water and microwave on high for 6 minutes. Drain and set aside.

Heat 3 tablespoons of the oil in a large saucepan/pot. Add the onions and cook over low heat for 3–5 minutes, until soft. Season with a little salt.

Add the (bell) peppers and cook for 5–8 minutes more, stirring occasionally. Season with a little salt.

Add 1 more tablespoon of the oil and then the courgettes/zucchini. Mix well and cook for 5 minutes more. Season with a little more salt.

Add 2 more tablespoons of the oil and the drained aubergines/eggplant. Cook, stirring often, for 5 minutes more. Add the tomatoes, 5 of the garlic cloves, half of the basil and 1 more tablespoon of the oil, if required. Check the seasoning and adjust if necessary. Cook for 5 minutes. Cover, reduce the heat and simmer gently for 30 minutes, stirring occasionally.

Stir in the remaining garlic and basil just before serving. Serve with rice or crusty bread, as preferred.

index